Secret World

By Greg V. Hurd

"Scripture quotations are from The ESV® Bible (The Holy Bible, English Standard Version®), copyright © 2001 by Crossway, a publishing ministry of Good News Publishers. Used by permission. All rights reserved."

Scripture taken from the New King James Version®. Copyright © 1982 by Thomas Nelson. Used by permission. All rights reserved.

THE HOLY BIBLE, NEW INTERNATIONAL VERSION®, NIV® Copyright © 1973, 1978, 1984, 2011 by Biblica, Inc.® Used by permission. All rights reserved worldwide.

Scripture quotations marked TPT are from The Passion Translation®. Copyright © 2017, 2018, 2020 by Passion & Fire Ministries, Inc. Used by permission. All rights reserved. ThePassionTranslation.com.

The Holy Bible, Berean Study Bible, BSB
Copyright ©2016, 2020 by Bible Hub
Used by Permission. All Rights Reserved Worldwide.

"Scripture quotations taken from the Amplified® Bible (AMPC), Copyright © 1954, 1958, 1962, 1964, 1965, 1987 by The Lockman Foundation. Used by permission. www.lockman.org"

"Scripture quotations taken from the Amplified® Bible (AMP), Copyright © 2015 by The Lockman Foundation. Used by permission. www.lockman.org"

"Scripture quotations taken from the (NASB®) New American Standard Bible®, Copyright © 1960, 1971, 1977, 1995, 2020 by The Lockman Foundation. Used by permission. All rights reserved. www.lockman.org"

Scripture quotations from The Authorized (King James) Version. Rights in the Authorized Version in the United Kingdom are vested in the Crown. Reproduced by permission of the Crown's patentee, Cambridge University Press

Scripture taken from the New King James Version®. Copyright © 1982 by Thomas Nelson. Used by permission. All rights reserved.

First Printing 2021

ISBN 978-1-7378124-1-8

Copyright © 2021 Treign Publishing All rights reserved.
Printed in the USA.

Inside Secret World

Housed within the souls of men and women, the Secret World is a metropolis constructed by the collective amalgamation of our thoughts, ideas, beliefs, and experiences. It houses the sum total of all of our personal happiness and fears. It is a bustling cosmogony of our tastes, preferences, and core values. It houses the personal beliefs we have about ourselves and others, and it houses the primary codex of our perceived world.

The Secret World is a substitute for the Secret Place. It was expressly designed by the adversary to obfuscate God and His Kingdom from the minds of fallen humanity. And to conceal, complicate, and confuse the plan of God from the believer.

Understanding the difference between the Secret World and the Secret Place is our burden and our obligation. We are called to work out our own salvation, to gain revelation in our spiritual lives. Then use that revelation to renew our souls and manifest it into our physical world. We are called to bring the truth of God's kingdom from our spirits and work that truth out until we are seeing the manifestations of His kingdom all around us.

TABLE OF CONTENTS

Secret World 1
Preface 11
Introduction:
Understanding the Secret World 15
SAME LOCATION, DIFFERENT WORLDS .. 23
MAN ON THREE DIMENSIONS 31
THE DOMINION MANDATE 37
Section 1: Building Cosmogony 45
COSMOGONY: The origin and development
of the universe/world 46
BLUEPRINTS OF COSMOGONY 53
BUILDING MATERIALS 56
THE CONTRACTOR'S TOOLS 64
CREATING COSMOPOLIS 73
Section 2: Surveying the Cityscape 85
HIGHWAYS AND BYWAYS 90
CARNAL CONSTRUCTIONS 100
CITY CULTURE 112
FORTIFYING YOUR CITY 118
Section 3: Taking Capitol Hill 141
UNRESTRAINED URBANIZATION 143
EMBASSY OF OFFENSE 148
DISMANTLING THE CITADEL OF PRIDE .. 150

Section 4: The Perilous Populace 159
ME TO THE POWER OF MANY 163
RESIDENTS OF INSPIRATION 167
ENEMIES OF THE STATE 170
Section 5: Invaders from Outer Space 173
GATEWAYS INTO THE CITY 175
SPIRITUAL VAGABONDS 182
THINGS THAT GO BUMP IN THE NIGHT .. 188
HIERARCHY OF THE MILITANT MINORITY 191
GANGS IN THE STREETS 197
LOOTING AND RIOTING 203
Section 6: Hardened Hearts of Concrete and Steel 207
WATCHING ASPHALT DRY 212
Section 7: City Shakedown 229
CITY STANDSTILL 233
THE DECONSTRUCTION CREW 238
UNATTENDED OVERGROWTH 244

Preface

They have healed the wound of my people lightly, saying "Peace, peace" when there is no peace.
Jeremiah 6:14, ESV

The contents of this book came from a place of personal pain and prayerful conviction. It would seem that the alchemy of revelation typically comes from this type of environment. Miracle rich territory often seems to be riddled with chaos and confusion, much to our disliking. In a recent season of my life in which I had been experiencing utter mayhem, the Lord began to stir my heart regarding these concepts. Through a personal crisis of my life, Jesus began to instill within me a greater sensitivity about the needs of people. He began to reveal his modes and methods both personally and professionally in my dealings with what was most important to Him: Humanity.

The scripture text at the head of this page served as a catalyst. Reading about the apostate priesthood in Jeremiah's day, and their apparent disregard for the things of God, and the service of God, flashbacks began projecting through my mind of instances in my dealings with people in which I was more concerned with fruit picking than root pulling. Times in which instead of diligently pursuing healing and restoration I was content with administering band-aids and cherry suckers.

In a book I was reading at the time, Derek Prince told the story of when he was a medical assistant in World War II. While he was assisting a battlefield doctor, an injured soldier came in with a piece of shrapnel in his side. The soldier had been hit by a grenade or a mortar shell, and there were also other small punctures on his body. As the doctor attended to the main wound, Prince noticed a small puncture in the soldier's shoulder and asked if he should get the gauze and bandage to cover it. The doctor answered in the negative and asked him to retrieve the probe and forceps instead. Although the puncture was very small and seemingly non-life threatening, the doctor jammed the probe into the wound, moving it in a circular motion until the wince of the wounded soldier indicated that he had connected with the tiny piece of shrapnel lodged deep in his flesh. He motioned for Prince to give him the forceps and immediately inserted them into the wound retrieving the tiny fragment.

When the shrapnel was removed, the doctor then instructed him to dress the wound.

Conviction swelled up inside of me as I recounted how many times I had concealed seemingly insignificant wounds of hurting people by wrapping them with the gauze, tape, and bandages of indifference. I had given quick quotes, pats on the back, and press-on prayers. How many times soldiers in the war of life had come into my timeline having been hit by the enemy's grenades and were wounded, hurting, and even despairing of life itself? In those times, my focus was on only what I could see with my naked eye, not what was hidden within. I began to lament over my desperate attempts to cover open wounds while not caring about the small punctures. This is easy to do because open wounds can make us really uncomfortable, we want to cover them as soon as possible without any regard for the person experiencing the pain in order to satisfy our own comfort level, leaving shrapnel that will eventually lead to more serious conditions. This is a travesty that has persisted for far too long in Christianity.

I began to see that I was comfortable with a church that ceased to be a hospital and was more content to track statistics and numbers. But Jesus began to birth in me a longing for a church that had blood on her floors, a church where people felt comfortable walking in their most vulnerable states, a place where gaping wounds were normal to see.

This gave birth to the revelation of the Secret World.

Introduction: Understanding the Secret World

"I stood in this sun sheltered place
Til I could see the face behind the face
All that had gone before had left no trace

Down by the railway siding
In our Secret World we were colliding
All the places we were hiding love
What was it we were thinking of?"

        Peter Gabriel, *Secret World*

Inside of each of us is a Secret World.

A place where deception and truth collide.

A place where our dreams can glide.

A place where all our thoughts and ideas reside.

A place where all our secrets try to hide.

A place where our enemies deride.

"Whoever is slow to anger is better than the mighty, and he who rules his spirit than he who takes a city."
                                          Proverbs 16:32, ESV

Solomon, writing under the inspiration of the Spirit of God states that the self-control of the emotions, in this couplet, anger, is better than the mighty and better than one who takes a city. Solomon connects the sensibility of anger with that of a city, comparing the soul with a metropolis that needs to be taken, subdued, and ruled. He goes on to state in Proverbs 25:28, ESV

"A man without self-control is like a city broken into and left without walls."

In both scriptures, the mind of man is likened to a city with all of its infrastructure and cosmogony. Which leads to the major truth of this book.

Housed within the souls of men and women, the Secret World is a metropolis constructed by the collective amalgamation of our thoughts, ideas, beliefs, and experiences. It houses the sum total of all of our personal happiness and fears. It is a bustling cosmogony of our tastes, preferences, and core values. It houses the personal beliefs we have about ourselves and others, and it houses the primary codex of our perceived world.

Now, we must not conflate the Secret World with the Secret Place. These are two very distinct realms. However, we can confuse the two if we are not aware of the differences, which is what I hope to explain in this book.

First, we must understand that the Secret World is a substitute for the Secret Place. Both are similar in function. Both boast a place of protection and acceptance, a place of escape from the ravages of the world. Both are centralized around a person. Both offer aid and comfort; however, they are diametrically opposites in the achievement of these promises.

> *He that dwelleth in the secret place of the most High shall abide under the shadow of the Almighty.*
>
> Psalms 91:1, KJV

The Secret Place is God-centric, the habitation of God within the believer, an intimate place of communion where God's heart and desires are shared, activated, and initiated. This place is housed within our spirit if we are born again and can be accessed any time.

If anyone loves me, he will keep my words, and my father will love him, and we will come to him and make our home with him.

John 14:23, ESV

For you have died, and your life is hidden with Christ in God.

Colossians 3:3, ESV

In him you also are being built together into a dwelling place for God by the Spirit.

Ephesians 2:22, ESV

The New Testament revelation of *God in us* is integral to understand if we are to differentiate between these two very powerful realms that both find their occupancy within us. This is a concept that is both incredibly complex and unusually simple.

Here are some primary differences to remember as we move forward:

1. The Secret Place is God-centric/The Secret World is self-centric.
2. The Secret Place is about the Kingdom of God/The Secret World is about our kingdom.
3. The Secret Place centers around the objectives of God/The Secret World is about our agenda.
4. The Secret Place is spiritual/The Secret World is soulical.
5. The Secret Place is substantive/The Secret World is fantasy.
6. The Secret Place is a place of truth/The Secret World can have both truth and deception.
7. The Secret Place has guarded access/The Secret World has open borders.
8. The Secret Place is for the spiritually minded/The Secret World is for the carnally minded.

As believers, the main onus of our struggles is the conflict between these two realms. Understanding the difference is our burden and our obligation. The goal of spiritual growth is for the Secret Place to take over and occupy the Secret World. This is referred to in the scriptures as mind renewal.

> *Do not be conformed to this world, but be transformed by the renewal of your mind, that by testing you may discern what is the will of God, what is good and acceptable and perfect.*
>
> Romans 12:2, ESV

> *That you put off concerning the former manner of life the old man, which is corrupt according to the deceitful lusts, and be renewed in the spirit of your mind; and that you put on the new man, which after God is created in righteousness and true holiness.*
>
> Ephesians 4:22-24, KJV-Scoffield

The Secret World was expressly designed by the adversary to obfuscate God and His Kingdom from the minds of fallen humanity and to conceal, complicate, and confuse the plan of God from the believer. His distortion of God's creation serves as the chief means of deception. He aims to create a cosmos brimming with contrarian information. Information that is meant to invoke a sophisticated captivity with invisible bars and transparent fences. A world that presents the mirage of endless possibilities and outcomes while concealing the true enslavement caused by the encouraged avarice.

SAME LOCATION, DIFFERENT WORLDS

One Wednesday night after Bible Study, as I walked to the front doors of our church chatting with my grandkids, I saw a disheveled figure scampering towards the entrance of the church. The service had been dismissed so I perceived this was a person who came with a great need. As the light finally revealed his face, I recognized him, greeted him, and asked how I could help him. He was in horrible shape. His facial contortions and the intermittent pulling out of his hair signaled that he was a man in distress. He walked back and forth as if he wanted to hastily turn back to his car and forget that he had ever arrived, but then he would turn back to me, his eyes crying for help like a prisoner in a cage. I sent my grandchildren with their parents then I proceeded to engage him in conversation. He was hesitant but desperate. Eager for help yet unwilling to accept it. There seemed to be an influence that was fighting for control. He stammered out duplicitous small talk as if there were multiple personalities vying for the helm. He looked at me with shame filled eyes and mouthed words with no sound. It was as if the real person was beating behind the lenses of his eyes crying to get free of this horrible nightmare! Being taken aback by this display I really did not know what to say, so passing over the obvious, I reflexively asked, "Sir, is everything ok?" Which is obviously a silly question in the face of so much evidence to the contrary. We stood outside on a beautiful summer night, both of us feeling the same 78 degrees weather, hearing the same stridulation of the locusts, standing underneath the same starry sky, standing at the same longitude and latitude, but we were in two completely different worlds!

I was immediately aware that what was going on the inside of him was far bigger than the 5'6" man that was standing before me. His Secret World was manifesting, seeking to dominate him and keep him from receiving deliverance. This was an extreme case, one that did not happen to this man overnight. The habitation had to be built to house these entities that tormented him. A city, built and fortified with a paved highway to its center, had been planned, executed, and constructed to bring this man to his knees. The building blocks of thoughts, images and ideas constructed the infrastructure needed for demonic habitation. What once was curiosity led to obsession, then to oppression, and then to demonization! The inhabitants of his city were rioting and holding him hostage!

Extreme as this incident was many people have varying degrees of demonic influence in their lives based upon their thoughts, images, philosophies, and beliefs.

> *Hereafter I will not talk much with you: for the prince of this world cometh, and hath nothing in me.*
>
> John 14:30, KJV

> *But each person is tempted when he is lured and enticed by his own desire.*
>
> James 1:14, ESV

Both Jesus and James state the same thing. In light of Jesus' ensuing time of crisis in which the enemy was coming for Him, He stated "the prince of this world is coming, but he does not have anything in me." In this statement Jesus is teaching that the way of victory is to live with zero resonance toward the enemy. James confirms that temptation comes to draw upon lusts that we have allowed to have unchecked access in our lives. Transient thoughts left to squat in our souls groom an appetite for things forbidden.

Satanic-implanted ideas, simmered in the soul of man, give birth to the aroma of desire until action is inevitable. We think in terms of fellowship as only with one another; however, we commune with our thoughts and ideas continually. They are cultivated, pruned, and fertilized based upon their appointed importance.

The carnal mind is open to these conditions, and that is why mind renewal is integral to the believer in developing a Spirit-controlled mind.

> *For those who live according to the flesh set their minds on the things of the flesh, but those who live according to the Spirit set their minds on the things of the Spirit. For to set the mind on the flesh is death, but to set the mind on the Spirit is life and peace. For the mind that is set on the flesh is hostile to God, for it does not submit to God's law; indeed, it cannot. Those who are in the flesh cannot please God.*
>
> Romans 8:5-8, ESV

This scripture states that:

1. The Carnal Mind is Body ruled
2. The Spirit Mind is Spirit ruled
3. We set our mind to either setting
4. The Carnal Mind produces Death
5. The Spirit Mind produces Life and Peace
6. The Carnal Mind is Hostile to God
7. The Spirit Mind is Hospitable to God
8. The Carnal Mind is lawless
9. The Spirit Mind fulfills the law

We must understand that the inner world (whether fleshly or spiritual) people are operating in can, at times, take over. When I interact with a person, I am not just dealing with carbon matter but with a very sophisticated and complex inner dimension. Just because it is unseen does not mean it is not real. Jesus dealt with this many times in the Gospels, and we will too if we seek to follow in His steps.

The Demoniac of Gadara comes to mind and how Jesus dealt with this demonized person who had a legion of demons inhabiting him (which is upward to 6,000). This story vividly illustrates that the enemy doesn't just want to only build a city within you, but to also populate it with tenants.

This man had a demonic population that dominated him to the point where he was no longer able to be in public but instead, he dwelt among the tombs.

> *They went to the other side of the sea to the region of the Gadarenes. When He had come out of the boat, immediately a man with an unclean spirit came out of the tombs and met Him. He lived among the tombs. And no one could constrain him, not even with chains, because he had often been bound with shackles and chains. But he had pulled the chains apart and broken the shackles to pieces. And no one could subdue him. Always, night and day, he was in the mountains and the tombs, crying out and cutting himself with stones. But when he saw Jesus afar off, he ran up and kneeled before Him, and cried out with a loud voice, "What have you to do with me, Jesus. Son of the Most High God? I adjure you by God, do not torment me." For Jesus said to him, "Come out of the man, you unclean spirit!" Then He asked him, "What is your name?" He answered, "My name is Legion. For we are many." And he begged Him repeatedly not to send them away out of the country. Now there was a great herd of swine feeding near the mountains. All*

the demons pleaded with Him asking, "Send us to the swine, so that we may enter them." At once, Jesus gave them leave. Then the unclean spirits came out and entered the swine. And the herd, numbering two thousand, ran wildly down a steep hill into the sea and were drowned by the sea.

Mark 5:1-13, KJV

When the demonized man saw Jesus, he didn't just casually walk to Him, he ran towards him, he rushed to Jesus. He threw himself down at Jesus' feet because he wanted to be free! Jesus did not address the man's countenance, his lack of clothes, or his desperate condition, He went directly to the Secret World and began to evict those demonic occupiers!

After the man is successfully delivered, the scriptures state that he was "clothed and in his right mind,"—the Greek word used here is *sophroneo* and it means to be "safety minded, exercising self-control, safely regulated, sober, to discipline passion, sound mind." One of the chief illustrations of this word is a diaphragm which regulates respiration, what comes in and what goes out of our lungs. "In his right mind "can be taken to mean that he now has control over his city and can regulate thoughts, ideas, and images in a way that does not open the door to infiltration. The goal of this teaching is to get you and keep you "of sound mind!"

MAN ON THREE DIMENSIONS

In Genesis we are told that we are created in the very image of God. This is foundational to understanding the triplicity of our lives. God himself is a three part being He is the divine trinity: Father, Son, and Holy Spirit. Likewise, we are made up of our spiritual life, our soul life, and our physical life. We are spirit beings, first and primarily. We have souls, and we live in bodies.

Now may the God of peace himself sanctify you completely, and may your whole spirit and soul and body be kept blameless at the coming of our Lord Jesus Christ.

1 Thessalonians 5:23, ESV

Human beings are tripartite. God's will is not just that our spirits are sanctified but that our entire person is sanctified. This scripture indicates that our complete self is three parts. These three parts are described by three separate Greek words. The first being *pneuma.* This is the word used for spirit. This refers to our innermost selves, the part of us that has been sealed by the Holy Spirit once we receive salvation. The second word used here is *psuché*, our soul. This consists of our mind, our will, and our emotions. The compilation of your spirit and soul is what makes up your heart. The third part of our lives mentioned in this verse is our *sóma*. Individually this refers to our physical bodies, and collectively it refers to the church, the body of Christ.

The primary drive and center of your nature is your Spirit. In Philippians we are commanded to work our spirits out.

Work out your salvation with fear and trembling.

Philippians 2:12b, ESV

Although this scripture has been taken out of context quite often, the reality of it holds great truth. We are called to work out our salvation. We are called to gain revelation in our spiritual lives, use that revelation to renew our souls, and then manifest it into our physical world. We are called to bring the truth of God's kingdom from our spirits and work that truth out until we are seeing the manifestations of His kingdom all around us. Our focus, however, is often quite contrary to God's intention for our lives because we don't fully understand who we are. Man is a spirit; you need to understand that humanity is a classification of spirit. You are not a human having a spiritual experience. You are a spirit, having a human experience.

In first Thessalonians chapter five and verse number 23, Paul says, "now may the God of peace sanctify you wholly" (ESV). Notice that God is the God of peace. This word comes from the Hebrew *shalom*. This word doesn't just mean peace of mind, but it refers to peace in every part of you. Did you know that the etymology of the word disease comes from dis-ease? Disease comes from the body not being at rest. It comes from the body not being in *shalom*, peace, but it's not just the body, it comes to every area of your life. God wants to bring peace to every aspect of your life, that's God's desire for you. Now, that does not mean you're not going to have problems. That does not mean that you're not going to have crisis situations. It just means that you can make the presence of God so prominent in your life, that it begins to cause you to be at peace in the midst of the storm. It means that the God of peace is greater than the storm!

Jesus spoke from that peace. When the storm came and he was out on the lake, he took that peace, and he released it into the storm. What happened? The storm ceased. He had control over what was going on around Him because God ruled all that was going on inside of Him. Jesus' inner life, His spirit man, gave way to manifestation of the Kingdom. God wants to bring that same peace to our lives, and it doesn't matter what is happening on the outside because greater is He that is in me (1 John 4:4). When God is put back on the throne of our Secret Worlds, the Prince of Peace is free to bring true restoration.

Our human focus tends to be on the outer man. If the outer man is comfortable and in convenience, we think that we have arrived, but nothing could be further from the truth. Your life can be going perfectly well, and your Secret World will be under siege. Due to the fact that our physical world is the one we engage in most consistently, we are dominated by its realities. What we fail to understand, however, is that each world is actually far more expansive than the last. Our physical world is the most minute and insignificant of the three. In 2 Corinthians 4, our bodies are compared to jars of clay. They are merely physical vessels that carry the treasure of our spirits. It is my hope that through this book you will be awakened to the depths and dominance of your spiritual world, the battlefield, and where the emphasis of the enemy is going to be.

What we fail to realize is that the enemy is a master strategist. Many have the misconception that the enemy is ignorant and foolish, but in truth he is quite clever. He knows the scripture better than most believers, and he knows that he cannot touch your spirit if you're born of God because the Greater One lives on the inside of you. But he also knows that he can manipulate you through your physical senses. He knows he can develop strongholds in the soul that keep the expression of the spirit from coming to manifestation by manipulating the way you perceive your experiences. The enemy seeks to build a Secret World in your heart. Remember, the spirit and the soul comprise what the Bible calls the heart. The physical heart has four chambers. The physical world often reflects the spiritual world, and the spiritual heart has four chambers also. The first chamber is your spirit, which is the hidden man of the heart (1 Peter 3:4). Remember that when Jesus died and rose again, he gave us the Holy Spirit. He breathed on us and sealed our innermost man. The other three chambers are your mind, your will, and your emotions, which are your sensibilities. All of these things work in unison together. When we are wholehearted, we release the Kingdom of God into our natural realm. When we have a divided heart, then our spirits are absolutely neutralized or powerless. This is exactly what the enemy seeks to do. He doesn't care if your name is written in the Lamb's book of life. He doesn't care if your name is written in heaven. He cares if you're going to connect your heart to God's. He cares if you have a complete and full heart because that means the kingdom of God can come through you. He wants to somehow short circuit that aspect of your life, and he does that by building things within your soul. This is where the war is waged, in the Secret World of man, in the cosmology of the soul.

THE DOMINION MANDATE

For we wrestle not against flesh and blood, but against principalities, against powers, against the rulers of the darkness of this world, against spiritual wickedness in high places.

Ephesians 6:12, KJV

Many Christians try to fight the battle through physical means. They try to wage war according to the flesh, but our fight is not one of flesh and blood. Our fight is spiritual, and our tactics must also be spiritual. It is important that we understand the soul is the battleground of the spiritual. Spiritual entities are waging war for supremacy of the soul. In Proverbs chapter 4 verse 23 Solomon advises, "Keep your heart with all vigilance, for from it flow the springs of life" (ESV). We are constantly being bombarded with all kinds of thoughts, attitudes, and accusations. The purpose of these things is to try to get you to develop a stronghold in your mind. The intention is for your desires to develop something in you that will enslave you (James 1:14,15). He wants to keep you from experiencing God's best. Here is what we must understand-the battle is not a fight for your life. The enemy doesn't care about you. He seeks to control your dominion. Satan wants to build something in your life to impair you and handicap you. He wants to keep you from achieving God's objectives for your life. He doesn't care if you get saved or not. It's really not a problem for him. Sure, he'd love to have you in hell, but that's really not the point.

He wants to do everything he can to neutralize you, and he'll put people in your life to accomplish this task. For example, you get into a relationship, and it's not the storybook thing that you thought it would be. It's not the high and lofty thing that you thought it would be, and it just doesn't go the way that you planned for it to go. Then you see someone else that does have what you want, and then you are attacked with an argument in your current relationship. All of the sudden the enemy takes that opportunity to begin to tell you the problem is you. He says to you, "You're the problem. No one cares for you. No one will ever love you. You're not going to have that kind of love; it is not for you." You begin to develop envy and jealousy, and it grows and begins to build a stronghold in your life to the point that you can no longer enjoy the happiness of others. Then you become constantly bitter and angry because people have what you feel you should have. The bitterness and anger lead to separation from God, and it gives the enemy more room to work, more land to develop.

My spiritual mother, Vivian Hines, used to say, "God doesn't like ugly." When we get ugly, the presence and the power of God is neutralized in our lives. It's not that he leaves, because he doesn't, he'll never leave you, he'll never forsake you. It's that we have put ourselves in a position in which we are not able to receive from His hand. The reason why people can't taste of the grace of God is because their city tells them it doesn't exist. This is exactly how the enemy builds strongholds that keep people from a loving God that wants to care for them and wants to nurture them and help them. He wants to keep you from God, so he can keep you from using your power.

> *And God said, Let us make man in our image, after our likeness: and let them have dominion over the fish of the sea, and over the fowl of the air, and over the cattle, and over all the earth, and over every creeping thing that creepeth upon the earth…And God blessed them, and God said unto them, Be fruitful, and multiply, and replenish the earth, and subdue it: and have dominion over the fish of the sea, and over the*

fowl of the air, and over every living thing that moveth upon the earth.

>   Genesis 1:26,28, KJV

In this verse, God delegates authority in the earthly realm to mankind. Man is given dominion over all of the creatures over the earth. Mankind is told to replenish and subdue the earth. The word subdue means to bring it under our subjection or to rule it. The unseen realm fights for the souls of men because that is where the dominion mandate resides. The execution of the dominion mandate is dependent on the spirit's control of the soul. Since the enemy has no access to your spirit, the only way he can gain control over your soul is through the manipulation of your flesh. This is why there is a constant war between the spirit and the flesh. They are both vying for control, and the victor will hold sway over the collective intellect, the driving sensibilities, and the dominant will of man.

> *walk by the Spirit, and you will not gratify the desires of the flesh. For the desires of the flesh are against the Spirit, and the desires of the Spirit are against the*

flesh, for these are opposed to each other, to keep you from doing the things you want to do.

Galatians 5:16-17, ESV

Each of us is in a constant battle. Our spirits wage war against our flesh, and our flesh wages war against our spirits. Their opposition causes internal turmoil and indecision. Now, it is vital to understand that our flesh is not the enemy. The problem isn't with our flesh but with how the enemy manipulates our flesh and rules us through it. Our flesh, just like our souls, needs to be conquered by our spirits. The enemy attempts to use the flesh to build an entire world of turmoil in your soul so that your spirit will be isolated, and you will have no authority in your life. He wants to be in control of your soul so that he can use your authority and giftings for his own purposes. The problem is most people don't even realize that he is doing this. The majority of people don't recognize the enemy's strategy.

We are not without hope though. God wants to teach us how to regain control over our hearts. Jesus died to give us our control back. He died so that we didn't have to fight alone, so that he could fight for us, and all we must learn to do is to live from His presence. One of our biggest problems is our lack of dependency on Him. We must begin this process with humility. The beginning of revelation is a humble heart. This requires vulnerability, but a lot of people don't desire to open themselves up. They want to wear their masks. and they want to stay behind their walls. Sure, they want to experience freedom, but, without surrender, freedom just isn't possible. Many people have not learned to trust God though. Many people have more distrust for God than they do for the voices in their heads. We must first realize that God is a good father, and He loves us with a greater love than anything we could comprehend with our own human intellect. We must realize that the presence of God is a safe environment to deal with unsafe things. Whatever happens in your life, God is ready and capable of dealing with it. For too long the enemy has hindered the people of God from breakthrough. Most people don't even believe they have anything to be free from, but each of us has a city inside of our souls. And our cities are under siege. There is a battle going on in our souls, a tug-of-war between our spirits and our flesh. I want to be free from war, and I want you to be free. It is my prayer that this book will give you the tools you need to be free. This is not a formula for change.

This is a blueprint for a complete overhaul of the Secret World that has been erected on the inside of you.

Section 1:
Building Cosmogony

COSMOGONY:
The origin and development of the universe/world

In the previous sections we discussed how we were created in the image of God. Having God himself as a prototype for our creation implies that we are created as three-part beings. What we have yet to discuss is the death of the spirit that occurred when Eve gave into sin. In Genesis chapter 3, Eve is presented with a choice, a choice that we are presented with every day. That choice is between what God says and what the enemy says. The passage goes as follows:

> *Now the serpent was more crafty than any other beast of the field that the Lord God had made. He said to the woman, "Did God actually say, 'You shall not eat of any tree in the garden'?" And the woman said to the serpent, "We may eat of the fruit of the trees in the garden, but God said, 'You shall not eat of the fruit of the tree that is in the midst of the garden, neither shall you touch it, lest you die.'" But the serpent said to the woman, "You will not surely die. For God knows that when you eat of it your eyes will be opened, and you will be like God, knowing good*

and evil. So when the woman saw that the tree was good for food, and that it was a delight to the eyes, and that the tree was to be desired to make one wise, she took of its fruit and ate, and she also gave some to her husband who was with her, and he ate.

Genesis 3:1-6, ESV

Now, many scholars debate whether this encounter included an actual serpent, or if it is just referring to Satan as a serpent. The word used for serpent here is the Hebrew word *Nachash,* which means the shining, glowing, enchanting, seducing one. Regardless of your opinion on this, the temptation presented was definitely from the enemy. When the serpent comes to Eve, whether a representative of Satan or Satan himself, he presents her with an alternative to the word of God, and for the first time, she is confronted with the counterfeit Secret World. This is always what the enemy attempts to do, he wants us to fall for a cheap imitation of good. The serpent planted doubt in Eve that led to her disobedience. Adam and Eve were given dominion over the earth in the previous chapters of Genesis, and the Devil wanted control of this dominion. Just as we discussed in the previous chapter, he is after our mandates. In order for him to have the full execution of the human tabernacle, which is the doorway to dominion, he had to get the tree of knowledge of good and evil in man, thereby creating an alternative, parallel cosmogony. He wanted to inject knowledge, or human reasoning, into the soul of man as a means of power, currency, leverage, and as a means of control.

The organic Eden and its agrarian principles were replaced with the concrete, asphalt, and steel of sense knowledge, human self-sufficiency, and self-preservation. Man would now need, or seek to replace, the purposes, passions, and securities inherent within them with a cheap imitation that provides a form but has no actual substance. With this act of manipulation, Satan began to create in man a new world order, one devoid of God's role as supreme. He brought death into a garden of life.

> *And you were dead in the trespasses and sins in which you once walked, following the course of this world, following the prince of the power of the air, the spirit that is now at work in the sons of disobedience— among whom we all once lived in the passions of our flesh, carrying out the desires of the*

body and the mind, and were by nature children of wrath, like the rest of mankind.

Ephesians 2:1-3, ESV

The word dead here is referring to the condition in which each of us existed before Christ. We were alienated from God. We were shut off from fellowship and intimacy. Our trespass was that we as humanity fell away from God after being close beside Him. Humanity took a false step that led to our separation from our heavenly father. We missed the mark, the standard which was set by our union with the holy one. The word used here for walked is the Greek word *peripateó*. This word means to habitually walk. This does not just imply a single fall or a single sin, but it implies the process of continually walking in a circuit contrary to God's divine intention.

This verse says, "following the course of this world." This is from the Greek word *Kata*, which means to come from a higher to a lower plane. This is to come down and come against the set order so as to put pressure on the individual. The order of this world is an order set to oppress.

This is used in Acts chapter 10 verse 38 when it says, "God anointed Jesus of Nazareth with the Holy Ghost and with power: who went about doing good and healing all that were oppressed of the devil; for God was with him" (KJV). This is the same word used for "oppressed" in this scripture. It is literally *Katadyivasteuomenous* which means to be oppressed and overpowered by a tyrant. The prince of the power of the air is the title given here for the one that is oppressing, for the tyrant that sets this present world order. This title is *Archonta Exousias Aeros*, or the ruler and authority of the lower air we breathe. His authority is a borrowed and lower authority, but the reason that he seems to have so much control in our life is because he understands how the system and kingdom of heaven works. Due to this, he is able to manipulate it especially for those without knowledge.

The enemy wants us to follow the course of the *Kosmos* (system or world order). His goal is to get us to walk in a circle under the oppressive force that instigates our set times and ideas that control our culture. The propagation of the ruler of the air, the spirit who is energizing the sons of disobedience, wants to manipulate our steps. Now the sons of disobedience are not just everyday nonbelievers. You don't get a title like that from an accidental slip up. These are people and spirits that willfully choose to not believe. These are those who refuse to be convinced, the obstinate and rebellious ones who stand in opposition to God's divine will. These are the ones who identify with the enemy. When we were dead in our trespasses, we lived in the desires of our flesh and our mind. We were children, by our very nature, of wrath. This verse is the culmination of the process that was initiated in Genesis chapter 3. In 2nd Corinthians we see the perpetuation of this new world order:

> But I am afraid that as the serpent deceived Eve by his cunning, your thoughts will be led astray from a sincere and pure devotion to Christ. For if someone comes and proclaims another Jesus than the one we proclaimed, or if you receive a different spirit from the one you received, or if you accept a different gospel from the one you accepted, you put up with it readily enough.
>
> 2 Corinthians 11:3-4, ESV

In these verses the Apostle Paul warns against this alternative world order. The injection of the tree of knowledge of good and evil is the other Jesus, the different spirit, the different gospel that he refers to. The enemy attempts to flip the world upside down. He wants to cause man to live from the outside in when we were created to live from the inside out. He desires for us to be controlled by our flesh rather than our spirits. He has essentially sought to flip our dominion. In the Secret World, the organic is replaced with the mechanic. His tactics are consistent and ancient, and they are also powerful. It is time we learn these tactics, so that we can begin to resist the enemy. Let us begin the journey of flipping our worlds right-side up.

BLUEPRINTS OF COSMOGONY

A personal worldview is the cognitive orientation that is fundamental to an individual. Experts say that our worldview begins to solidify around the age of 14. This means that by the age of 14 years old the majority of people will have their city pretty much up and running. At this point in people's lives, they actually believe that the way they see the world is the way the world should be seen. Now I am not an expert, but I have raised 4 boys, and trust me, their minds have all been just about made up by that point. Anyone reading this who has teenagers can attest to this. When they get into those adolescent years, they begin to immediately know better than everyone else. Have you talked to a 14-year-old recently? They pretty much have what they want to do in life planned out, and their beliefs are the end all, be all of truth. They know how they feel about things, and most have a pretty solid understanding of themselves.

Now the majority of our development is not done through teaching. Although words act as building blocks, the blueprint for our city is not built through words or didactic methods. The majority of us build the foundation of our cities through example. If we see certain things in the home, then we make room for these things in our cities. If we don't see certain things in the home, then those things will not become prioritized. For example, if you grow up in a house that prioritizes prayer, then prayer becomes a pivotal part of your life; likewise, if you grow up in a house that lacks affection and love, then you will not leave room for those things in your city. The blueprint for the foundation of our city is developed through modeling, through example. This is the reason that the devil has so adamantly attacked the nuclear family. He has attempted to remove the father from the house, so that he could interrupt our connection with the Heavenly Father. He has attempted to take away the sanctity of marriage, so that we won't understand what the church's marriage to the Lamb should look like. He wants to totally destroy and annihilate it because if there's no proper blueprint, then our inner man is constructed in chaos. And if there's no blueprint, then not only will the enemy be able to build us, but he'll be able to control our mandate.

Now, by the time we are adults, the majority of us have the blueprint for our city set. The blueprint comes in the forms of beliefs. Now there are two types of beliefs that are fundamental to the development of your city's blueprint. The first type is fact. These are things that have been proven to be true, things that we see as undeniable. The second is preference. Our preferences are determined by our own tastes and opinions. These are usually rooted in comparisons. The third type of belief is ideology. Ideologies reflect the patterns we see around us. Each of these beliefs, although not seen with the physical eye, are effectual motivators of actions and decision making.

The blueprints that your belief system creates established boundaries in your city. You relegate information based on one of the types of belief and give them weight based on their position. The problem with this is that any belief system that is not built on the foundation of Christ is wrong. When we live from the Secret Place and not the Secret World, our blueprints are destroyed, and the word of God becomes our basis for truth, preference, and ideology.

BUILDING MATERIALS

If you are a contractor or have any knowledge about the way that buildings are constructed, you know that, after the blueprints are decided on, the next task is to gather the materials needed to build. You cannot hope to start construction if the materials are not gathered. The enemy knows this too, so if our beliefs become the blueprints for our city, then what is it that becomes the building materials?

In the beginning, God created the heavens and the earth. The earth was without form and void, and darkness was over the face of the deep. And the Spirit of God was hovering over the face of the waters. And God said...

Genesis 1:1-3, ESV

As God built the spiritual (the heavens) and the physical (the earth), He created with His voice. "God said..." and so it was. This is the method God chose for creation, and this is one of the primary methods that is used to build our Secret World as well. Like our father, we have been given the power of creation within our words. This is true for the physical, we are able to make confessions in faith and see things come to pass, but it is also true in our soul realm. Words are the most significant building blocks of our Secret World. They are the nucleus of all life. We are a collection of words- words spoken, heard, believed, doubted, and received.

Did you know that, on average, people speak around sixteen thousand words a day? It is true, and regardless of whether you are male or female, the statistic stands. Apart from the things we say, research shows that the average person hears around thirty thousand words a day (Huynh). That is almost double. What this tells me is that things are being built in us at an extremely fast rate. This is why the people you surround yourself with are so important. So many of us surround ourselves with voices that are constantly hurling ideologies, beliefs, and arguments that are contrary to the truth of Jesus Christ. We consume these words that are thrown at us at a rapid pace, and this input starts to bog us down. Understand that the enemy uses these words to get a foothold into the door of your heart. He uses the books you read. He uses your favorite television program. He uses your favorite news media outlet. He uses your teachers and professors. He uses your bosses and leaders. He even uses those that you love and respect.

This is why God warns against the misuse of our words so many times throughout the Bible. When we use our words to lift, we can restore and heal with those words, but when we are careless with our words, they can be dangerous to the hearer.

> *Do not let any unwholesome talk come out of your mouths, but only what is helpful for building others up according to their needs, that it may benefit those who listen.*
>
> Ephesians 4:29, NIV

The word used in this passage for building is the Greek word *oikodomé*. This word means to build architecture as a suitable dwelling place, or temple, for God. If edifying words can be used to restore the temple in our hearts, then it makes sense that destructive words can be used to build temples or dwelling places to false gods. Our words and the words we hear can be used as the materials to build monuments to pride, hatred, bitterness, and fear. They can alter the geography of our souls and create strongholds for the enemy to live in. A stronghold is an area that is strongly fortified and easily upheld. When the enemy creates strongholds in our hearts, they become very difficult and painful to remove. A single word does not typically have the ability to create a monument or a stronghold in our Secret World, but as we are inundated with a plethora of words and similar words, they stick together and manufacture the media used in the creation.

Additionally, the enemy uses our emotions as building materials. Now I don't want you to misunderstand, emotions are not always bad. God gave us emotions as a gift. They are the way we connect the things we are experiencing with our souls; however, emotions are meant to be ruled and not to rule over us. When emotions become our masters, the enemy has free reign to come in through the door that we have opened. He begins to lie, deceive, and manipulate our emotions in order to use them to gain access to our hearts. He uses them to solidify and fortify the buildings that are under construction in our Secret Worlds. Information that is felt solidifies far more rapidly because it bypasses reasoning and goes straight to the heart. When we are not in control of our emotions, they dictate our world view by strengthening the monuments that obstruct it. Emotions are dangerous navigators because they will always guide us to discover whatever information is necessary to validate their existence.

Now, when we use our spirits to rule our emotions, they can become powerful tools for interacting with the world around us. When we seek God and ask Him how he feels about circumstances, then they can become connectors and even instruments of worship. Just like words, it is all dependent on whose hands they are in. When in God's hands, they can be used to beautify the inside of our temples, but when in the enemy's hands, they can be used to strengthen the self-centered monuments we create. How can we make sure that our words and emotions remain in the right place?

> *In all circumstances take up the shield of faith, with which you can extinguish all the flaming darts of the evil one .*
>
> Ephesians 6:16, ESV

This scripture lays out the tactic of the enemy. He launches and hurls fiery darts, or arrows, at us. The picture here is a soldier being bombarded by a plethora of arrows all at once. Paul makes a unique specification here, and that is with the use of the word flaming. The practical implication of lighting an arrow on fire is so that it doesn't just inflict the primary damage, but it also has the capacity to bring further damage with time. These arrows don't just inflict a wounding blow, but they also burn their recipients. The enemy uses words and emotions like flaming arrows. He throws them at us and bombards us with them, so that we are overwhelmed under the weight of their power. He uses quantity to make up for his lack of true strength. He uses undercutting remarks, and like the master strategist he is, he hurls emotions that will cut the deepest. He throws the language that your abusive father used on you. He disrupts you with dialogue that your ex used when she/he decided to leave, and he stirs that same feeling in you every time you try to get close to someone again. He brings up past hurts, rejections, and heartbreaks. He uses verbiage that reminds you of your lost loved ones because he doesn't just want to inflict a wounding blow, but he wants them to continue to burn in us long after we receive them.

    Although this scripture reveals the tactic of the enemy, it also reveals the solution for resisting these fiery darts. The solution is the shield of faith. The problem is that most of us don't use our faith to combat the enemy's words.

This is because the enemy's input into our lives far outweighs God's input. We watch 4 hours of television, and we spend 15 minutes with God. We spend every weekend hanging out with our friends, but if church goes 2 minutes past noon, then we are walking out. We dedicate ourselves to our jobs, but we can't find the motivation to spend time in God's word. We are so content with hearing all of the voices that bombard us every day that we fail to seek out His voice. We are so busy hearing from men that we forget to seek the voice that matters most. The media, our friends, our bosses, our circumstances have the power to dictate the way that we feel, but we've never given God that option. Our hearts break when our favorite sports team loses, but they don't break for the lost. We experience excitement when we get our Christmas bonuses but feel lifeless when the opportunity arises to give to our provider.

So faith comes from hearing, and hearing through the word of Christ.

Romans 10:17, ESV

The word used for hearing (*akoe*) is in the Greek perfect tense. This implies a repetitive cycle of hearing that never ends. The prescription for resisting the attack of the enemy is faith, and the prescription for receiving faith is the repetitive hearing of the word of God. Words are the very foundation, the nucleus, of all we see around us and all that is built within us. This is true regardless of where the words come from; however, the words of God have a greater power to build and destroy than any other because the words written in the Bible are backed by the very authority of heaven. We must become people of His word. We must become people who are constantly consuming the things of God, so that we are not consumed by the things of the world.

THE CONTRACTOR'S TOOLS

Have you ever asked yourself, why don't I do what I know I need to do? Why am I just continuing to trip over this same habitual thing in my life? Why does it always happen at this time of the year? Why do I have this problem? Why do I have to make everybody else ugly, so I can feel good about myself? Why do I have to cut other people off at the legs, so that I can feel secure and safe and feel good about myself? Why is that? Well, it has to do with the Secret World. It has to do with the city within. Although all words have the capacity to build, the enemy manipulates words in certain ways to begin construction of the city in your Secret World.

> *For though we walk in the flesh, we are not waging war according to the flesh. For the weapons of our warfare are not of the flesh but have divine power to destroy strongholds. We destroy arguments and every lofty opinion raised against the knowledge of God, and take every thought captive to obey Christ, being ready to punish every disobedience, when your obedience is complete .*
>
> 2 Corinthians 10:3-6, ESV

What are the contractors using? What is being used to build this city inside of you? The three tools used for building that are outlined here are arguments, lofty opinions, and thoughts. First off, he's using arguments. Arguments is the Greek word *logismos,* and it means reasoning, thought, conception, and to personally assign value to particular arguments. This is reasoning based on your personal values. We are constantly in a state of quarrel, did you know that you are constantly arguing with yourself? "I should have done this." "I shouldn't have got these donuts." "I need to go get a power bar and not eat these donuts." You exist in a constant state of arguing, and your inner workings are beginning to gauge and give value to certain thoughts. Did you know that you're arguing with something within yourself almost every single moment of the day? When certain things don't match up, when certain people don't see things the way that you see them, you begin to argue within yourself. You're constantly going back and forth between contrary ideas. An argument assigns value to a thought. We are constantly bombarded with all this information and stimuli from all around us, and it comes at us at a feverish pace. This fosters arguments. We begin to argue within ourselves between beliefs we once held and the new information we are being presented with. We are arguing, wrestling, "we are doing that, and they shouldn't be doing this, or they should be doing that." This is true when operating in the workplace when certain things are not how we expect them to be or when we are caught off guard and our rhythm is interrupted. What happens? An argument goes off on the inside of us!

We begin to construct things with these arguments. We begin to build how we feel about the person we're dealing with and about the company we are operating under. We begin to make decisions and pass judgements. We are making decisions that will assemble a paradigm, and if we don't deal with it, it could become permanent. The Bible states in Ephesians 4:27 "and give no opportunity to the devil." (ESV) The King James Version translates it this way, "Neither give place to the devil." The Greek word used for opportunity in the ESV and place in the KJV is *topos* where we get our English word for topography. This describes the mapping of an area or a piece of land and its layout. We are commanded by the Apostle Paul in this scripture to not allow the devil to gain access over our topography, our real estate. We need to see inner arguments as a form of bartering over soulical real estate, and we should never allow the enemy's contractors to gain a building permit on the soil of our heart!

Our perceptions of entire people groups can be altered by an argument that we allowed to form into concrete. There are women that are married to men yet hate men because they have allowed arguments to build a constructed habitation of hatred within them. There are men that distrust women, but yet are married to them. They allowed arguments to lay the groundwork for deep suspicion and wariness within them. There are people that absolutely hate what they do, but they show up every Monday and don't think they have the ability to do anything else because they've argued themselves out of their destinies.

Notice the next thing used as building materials, every lofty opinion. This is the Greek word *hupsóma*. These are things elevated in opposition to God. This is when you choose to give more importance to what you think, or to what others think, than to what God thinks. These lofty opinions are continuing to try to lay asphalt on top of what God is trying to grow in your life. If you'll allow Him to, God will grow grass through that asphalt, but when we don't take care of business, the demonic forces that are influencing our city and taking over various areas of our lives will begin to stamp out any green growth. What God does is always green. He's always organic. What man does and what the enemy does is not organic, it's superficial. It's manufactured. What's on the inside of us has been manufactured through arguments and through lofty opinions.

Then Paul talks about thoughts. The word used for thoughts here is the Greek word for knowing, *noéma*. This simply means the workings and musings of the mind. It can also mean "mind games." In 2 Corinthians 2:11 Paul states,

"So that we would not be outwitted by Satan; for we are not ignorant of his designs" (noemata).

This scripture is written in the context of offense which is one of the number one contractors that build in our minds. The lure of unforgiveness and offense is subtle and can be self-justifying. But this is a mind game to open access to the enemy to begin building a fortification in our city. A monument, if you will, dedicated to said offense that can endure our entire lifetime! We must be wise and identify Satan's mind tricks by continuing in the Word of God and crying out to the Father for discernment.

So how are these things built? As we saw with offense, the enemy brings in certain stimuli to get us into the realm of argument, to get us in the realm of opinion, to get us in the realm of thought, so that construction begins on the inside of us, and we begin to get presupposed ideas about what's going on around us. These things seek to snuff out the Word of God, to build over the green grass that has been sown. Now we've got buildings all around, and they are filled with all kinds of information. They are filled with all of our life experiences, all of our own ideas and opinions. This is my city, and in my city, I am always right, and I always have the final say. I am the center of my city; it is named after me after all.

> *See to it that no one takes you captive by philosophy and empty deceit, according to human tradition, according to the elemental spirits of the world, and not according to Christ.*
>
> Colossians 2:8, ESV

Here we have more tools used by the enemy for construction, tools that are used to take us captive. The first is philosophy or the Greek word *philosophia*. This is the love of human wisdom. More specifically, this is to elevate human wisdom over God's wisdom. It is a reflection of mankind's initial sin which is steeped in pride. When Adam and Eve ate from the tree of the knowledge of good and evil, they birthed human wisdom. We are being convinced by the spiritual entities trying to build our cities that our wisdom, man's wisdom, is higher than God's.

The second tool used in this scripture is the Greek words *kenēs apatēs*, empty deceit. Literally, this is a false impression that winds up being empty and vain. The impression, or delusion, is used in order to cheat and deceive. It is high-sounding nonsense; the mastery of verbiage inclines you to listen and believe, but in actuality, it has no substance. This is rooted in the idolatry of knowledge. The purpose of both of these tools is to take the deceived captive or *sulagógeó*. By implication, the enemy wants to make you a victim of fraud. He wants to carry off the treasure that is on the inside of you, that is Christ Jesus. He uses the seduction of pride and idolatry in order to erect buildings in your heart.

The scripture goes on to say that this is "according to human tradition." These are things that have been transmitted to us from generations passed. Practices, beliefs, or ideas that have been passed down that limit our connectivity to God. Your traditions are deceiving you into settling for less than God has created you to be. This is done according to the elemental spirits of the world, or the *kosmos*. This word for world doesn't refer to all that has been created, but it refers to the false ordered system that is a part of your Secret World. These elemental spirits are manipulators of the rudiments with which mankind has been indoctrinated.

What I want you to see is that you are a complex individual. There are far more complexities and nuances to you than you would ever even realize. The enemy is able to infiltrate and begin to cause these strongholds to be stabilized into massive structures, into buildings. He deploys entities to guard them. Any thoughts, any ideas, any messages, or anything with the anointing of God is denied access because it has the power to obliterate that city.

There is a whole world inside of you. The blueprints are your belief systems. The materials used for construction are words and emotions, and the tools in the hands of the satanic contractor are deceits and manipulations. We've got a lot of work to do because these buildings aren't coming down by themselves. We have to purposefully renew our mind to the word of God and demolish our Secret Worlds with His word.

CREATING COSMOPOLIS

As we have previously established, the enemy has one primary goal, and that goal is to separate humanity from the Father who loves them dearly. The primary way that he seeks to accomplish this goal is through the building of the Secret World. He wants to create Secret Worlds in each of us that he has dominion over, so that he can, in turn, create an intrinsic one-world system that operates independent of God. The natural fallen man will inevitably build a city within themselves. This is because both the collective populace and the fallen human soul have one objective: Cosmopolis.

In W. Warren Wagar's, *The City of Man*, he explains:

> "Cosmopolis means, simply, from the Greek 'world city.' The world-city (*Romans 12:1-2*) is the inevitably large spiritual and intellectual and administrative capital of civilization (apart from God), of the whole civilized world, or, more broadly, it is the quintessence of a civilization, the gathering of all its vital human resources into a living organic unit... Cosmopolis is simply the world in a state of optimal integration" (Wagar 15).

People tend to mistake this for a good thing. When they hear "world peace" or "world unity," it sounds like a positive thing, but the goal of the enemy is to create a one-world system that is separate from God. Satan is building a kingdom to oppose God, and since man has been given all of the creative authority in the earth, Satan has to go through man in order to establish it. In order to build anything physically, he must first build it within man's heart. This is the same way that God chose to manifest His Kingdom on the earth.

Based on the rules of Biblical interpretation, specifically the principle of first mention, it is essential for us to understand this topic from the point that it is first introduced in scripture. The first person we see in scripture to be manipulated into establishing their own city is Cain, the son of Adam and Eve. If you remember the story of Cain and Abel, we can establish the foundation of the building of his city. The story of Cain and Abel takes place in Genesis chapter 4. They are brothers who both had relationship with God. As the story goes, each of them brought a sacrifice to God, and God was pleased with Abel's sacrifice over Cain's because Abel's sacrifice came from a place of love. It was the very best that Abel had to offer. God was not, however, pleased with Cain's sacrifice because he did not give a sacrifice from a place of love or devotion, but merely obligation. God's favor towards Abel's sacrifice caused Cain to be enraged with anger and jealousy, and it eventually led to Cain murdering his brother. When God uncovered what Cain had done, he punished Cain through the curse of not being able to grow on the soil that he possessed. In sin, Cain lost the ability to live in the land outside of the Garden of Eden, which is a physical representation of the secret place (the ideal place for Christians to live from). He was forced, by his disobedience, to leave this land. Due to this, Cain decided to establish his own city which was *east of eden*.

> Then Cain went away from the presence of the Lord and settled in the land of Nod, east of Eden. Cain knew his wife, and she conceived and bore Enoch. When he built a city, he called the name of the city after the name of his son, Enoch.
>
> Genesis 4:16-17, ESV

The first thing we see in this scripture is that Cain went away from the presence of the Lord. This was an intentional act that left him in a vulnerable position. When we choose to venture out from the umbrella of the Lord's divine purpose for our lives, we become vulnerable and susceptible to the tactics of the enemy. Cain decided to dwell in the land of Nod, which translates to the place of wandering. Many people believe that he had no other option but to leave, but the truth is quite contrary. Cain had the ability to trust in God for his provisions instead of trusting in his own strength. Cain chose to rely on his own abilities instead of trusting in God's provision. Due to this decision, he no longer had a dwelling place with the Lord, but instead dwelt in a land where he could find no peace. When he built this first city named after his son Enoch, he established a precedent for the first Secret World. He manifested in the physical, through the building of this city, what was already present in his soul. With the establishment of this city, he built a world that was centered around him and his family. The city he built was a place where he was all powerful. In this city, he established his own justice that stood in opposition to the will of God. Through the creation of this city, he was seeking to fill the void in his spirit that was left by God's absence, more correctly by his departure from God's presence.

In *The Meaning of the City*, Jacques Ellul describes this process in great detail, stating,

> "Cain will satisfy his desire for security by creating a place belonging to him, a city. The city for Cain is first of all the place where he can be himself... His homeland is the one settled spot in his wanderings. Second, it is a material sign of his security. He is responsible for himself and for his life. He is far from the Lord's face, and so he will shift for himself... The city is the direct consequence of Cain's murderous act and of His refusal to accept God's protection...Such is the act by which Cain takes his destiny on his own shoulders, refusing the hand of God in his life" (Ellul 5).

Cain establishes a city that acts as a substitute for the Garden of Eden, a substitute for the Secret Place. This city system was all about what Cain could do, and what he believed was right in his own eyes. He set his own morals, beliefs, and wants over the plans and purposes of God.

> *For this is the message that ye heard from the beginning, that we should love one another. Not as Cain, who was of that wicked one, and slew his*

> brother. And wherefore slew he him? Because his own works were evil, and his brother's righteous...Hereby perceive we the love of God, because he laid down his life for us: and we ought to lay down our lives for the brethren.
>
> 1 John 3:11-12,16, KJV

In this passage we are given two options for the course of humanity. The first option is one devoid of love. It is one filled with pride, jealousy, and anger. It is one that promotes self over others and seeks to acquire more power. It is the path of Cain. The man who went away from the presence of God and built his own city. Contrarily, there is the path of Christ. The path of Christ is marked by self-sacrifice, love, and humility. It is a path that lives from the Secret Place and refuses to build a city of the soul that stands in opposition to the kingdom of God.

In reference to the city built by Cain, Ellul goes on to say,

> "Now a start is made, and it is no longer God's beginning, but mans. And thus Cain, with everything he does, digs a little deeper the abyss between

himself and God. There was a solution for his situation, but the solution was in God's hands, and that is what he could absolutely not tolerate. He wants to find alone the remedy for a situation he created, but which he cannot himself repair because it is a situation dependent on God's grace" (Ellul 6).

Cain did not obtain the humility that was necessary to remain in the Secret Place. He wanted to be independent from God, so that he could do whatever he wanted to do. This is where many believers find themselves. They acquire the mental assent that God is real, but they do not have the humility necessary to pursue His ultimate will for their lives. They don't want to be out of control. They are unwilling to give up their power, and they don't understand that their true power would be amplified by surrendering to God's ultimate authority.

The name of the first city was Enoch which means to initiate. In this instance, the city of Enoch initiates a new world order that is devoid of God. A city that is godless and ruled by man. Cain, like most of us, sought to build a place that he could reside and feel at home; however, when we attempt to build a home that isn't centered around God, we will never find rest.

Another person that is shown establishing his own city is Nimrod. Nimrod was the great grandson of Noah, and he was a mighty hunter. He was considered a mighty man of old. He was a rebel, and he chose to rebel against the order of God. He was a powerful man who became a city builder. Unlike Cain, he did not stop at just one city. Nimrod built an entire kingdom, an entire world, that was based on this Secret World.

In Genesis it says,

> *His kingdom began in Babylon, Erech, Accad, and Calneh, in the land of Shinar. From that land he went forth into Assyria, where he built Nineveh, Rehoboth-Ir, Calah.*
>
> Genesis 10:10-11, BSB

This scripture demonstrates the vastness of the kingdom he created. This kingdom led to the creation of one of the most infamous cities in the Bible, Babel. Babel became what we know as the kingdom of Babylon which was one of the biggest oppositions to the children of Israel in the Old Testament. The name Babylon comes from the

Akkadian *bav-ilim,* which means "the gates of the gods," and so this city became the gateway for the lesser gods of the earth to interact with mankind (Psalm 82). The emphasis of this city was self-worship, the worship of humanity. The thing that most people do not realize is that Satan doesn't have to get people to worship him in order to establish a one-world system. His task is much simpler. He just has to siphon the worship that belongs to God. As long as it is not going to God, he is satisfied. He can do this by getting people to worship self, or culture, or another individual. It really doesn't matter because if you are not for God, you are against Him. If the kingdom you are establishing is not God's kingdom, it is the enemy's. There is no neutral ground. We are always worshipping something; this is why there are so many genres of music. Some music tries to get you to bow a knee to your emotions, some to money, and others to romantic love. Each type of music is a conduit of worship. This doesn't mean that all music is evil by any means, but it does direct our worship, so we should be cautious of that.

Through the building of Babel, Satan employed man's worship of self. One of the most eerie examples of this is found in Genesis when the people of Babel say,

Come, let us build for ourselves a city, and a tower whose top will reach into heaven, and let us make for ourselves a name, otherwise we will be scattered abroad over the face of the whole earth.

Genesis 11:4, NASB

I say this passage is eerie because this is an extreme example of the thought process that rules the minds of most of humanity. The part that especially resonates is "let us make for ourselves a name." This phrase is the driving factor behind many of man's ambitions, it is the reason that people strive to be successful; however, a friend of mine once told me that true success is only measured in obedience to God. I believe this to be true. All of man's natural ambitions are but vain counterfeits of God's intended purpose for our lives. When we seek to chase after those ambitions, we are left scattered and unfulfilled. Our lives lack any true contentment. The building of the city of Babel, later Babylon, is one of the most transparent biblical examples of the way that Satan works in our Secret Worlds. He gets his hooks into our heart and begins to twist and twist until we are just a shadow of what God intended for us to be. He works us over until we begin to manifest things that are contrary to the very One who created us. He uses us for his own agenda, the creation of Cosmopolis.

Many of us, just like Nimrod, were given giftings by God. These giftings were not intended to serve Self. They were intended to serve God, but when the Secret Place is exchanged for a Secret World, giftings are kidnapped and used for the advancement of cosmopolis. The organics of the Secret Place are replaced with the mechanics of the Secret World. These concepts are hidden from most of humanity. The intents and purposes of the enemy's manipulation of your life are hiding in the shadows. Without knowledge, people perish (Hosea 4:6). When we stay unaware of the enemy's goals for humanity, we perish. His attack on you is not about you. It is about utilizing your creative power to establish cosmopolis and counteract kingdom manifestations.

Section 2:
Surveying the Cityscape

In the previous sections, we have discussed the complex nature of man, and how this nature affects our day to day lives. We have talked about the strategy of the enemy, and how he uses our beliefs, our words, our emotions, and specific types of manipulations in order to develop a layout and begin construction of a city inside your Secret World. I am using this metaphor of a city to further your understanding of what our Secret Worlds look like. The basis of learning is rooted in metaphor, and when we as human beings have something that we are familiar with to compare our new knowledge to, we develop a more deeply rooted understanding of the concept. This is demonstrated in the teachings of Jesus. As Jesus attempted to teach the mysteries of heaven to his disciples, He spoke through parables or allegories that were used to give the disciples a basis for comparison. For this purpose, I have chosen to use an extended metaphor in order to fully explain this concept. I do not intend to imply that natural cities are bad, nor is this an appeal to get people to live a more rural lifestyle. The purpose is to simply show that the enemy wants you to create a city opposed to the Secret Place. He wants to present you with a counterfeit to God's heavenly dwellings, so that you are ineffective in this earth.

> *Your kingdom come, your will be done, on earth as it is in heaven.*
>
> Matthew 6:10, ESV

Jesus is showing the disciples, and us all, through this scripture that one of our greatest and most primary focuses as believers should be to manifest the kingdom of heaven in the earth. When Jesus was baptised in the Jordan River, the heavens were opened over him, and when the heavens opened, they never closed again. In that moment, Jesus and all of his followers were granted access to the kingdom of God, and they were given an open door. Our job is to step through that door and bring the kingdom back with us, to establish His kingdom in our world. But if the enemy can get us to manifest our own kingdoms instead, if he can get us to build a Secret World (complete with our very own city), then he can disrupt this focus. When Adam and Eve listened to the serpent in the Garden, they were made susceptible to the very same spirit that influenced Satan. The spirit of *nachash,* the spirit of the enemy. This spirit is responsible for the manipulation of God's creation. When Eve ate of the forbidden fruit, she submitted herself to this spirit. In that moment, she expelled the spirit of God and replaced it with the spirit of sin and death. She exchanged the Secret Place for the Secret World. So many Christians live lives devoid of kingdom manifestation, and this is because we have exchanged the Secret Place with our Secret World. Understanding the geography of our Secret Worlds, our cities, will help us to navigate the difference because often the cities we build inside ourselves obstruct our view of God's will. Through the examination of our cityscape, we will all be given the tools necessary for city deconstruction.

In order for change to occur in the life of a believer, we must first get the revelation that there is a problem. In order for God to cleanse us, we must first be made aware of the strongholds that have been built inside our hearts. The divine surgeon cannot work inside of us, unless we give Him permission. He cannot remove anything that we choose to keep. He has transferred his authority on the earth to us, so we must recognize the problem and see the singular solution which is Jesus Christ in us. We must recognize what makes up our cityscapes, so that we can give access to the Lord. He can and will tear down every wall that keeps us from experiencing the fullness of His glory, but he must first have access to it.

A cityscape is the visual appearance of a city or urban area, a city landscape. In this section, I hope to give you a clearer image of what our cities actually consist of, the sectors that are found in our cities, and the strongholds we have created that limit God's ability to operate through us. My intention is to give you a survey of your cityscape because I believe if we can understand the geography of the world that is inside of us, we can begin to recognize the need for a complete overhaul. In that recognition, we can find true and long-lasting freedom.

HIGHWAYS AND BYWAYS

Fragmentation of mind, irrational thoughts, and convoluted thinking all arise from a mind that is being manipulated to create cosmopolis. This mind is opened to being molded by the world system, deceitful spirits, and the doctrines of demons. The fruit of a mind that is creating cosmopolis is fear, anxiety, stress, and worry. We know this is contrary to Jesus because 2 Timothy 1 verse 7 says "for God gave us a spirit not of fear but of power and love and self-control" (ESV). When our minds are not producing power, love, and self-control, we can assume that it is because there is some construction in our Secret World that is obstructing our view and ability to experience the fullness of the gospel.

Continuing our metaphor, our inner worlds are likened to a city, and just like physical cities, our cities have various means of travel. In a natural city, roads are the means by which its inhabitants travel. If any natural city is going to be successful, there has to be a way to get around in it. These roads improve access to the parts of your city. A successful city has highways, main roads, and even backroads. The roads, and our city's transportation district, are ruled by the mind, and the enemy is a master manipulator of the mind.

The enemy has no physical voice, he has no real power, so he fights us the only way he truly can, and that is through manipulation. He manipulates your thoughts and fights on the battlefield of the mind. He convinces us to believe things about people and about ourselves that keep us from experiencing the best in life. When we have been burned by an ex-girlfriend or boyfriend, he convinces us to keep people at arm's length because we are just going to get burned again. When we have been abandoned by a parental figure, he immediately manipulates us into developing a disregard and distrust for authority figures. When we have been forgotten by a friend, he tries to get us to believe that no one can love us, at least not long term. I know that these things are relatable to each of us, we all have to battle them, whether consciously or subconsciously. They pave roads in our souls that take us places we never intended to go. When these things become repetitious, the process of overcoming them becomes even more challenging. The frequency of travel determines the quality of the road. This is why our soul has many types of roads that run through it.

The first type of roads that are in our cities are the backroads. These roads are the oldest pathways that we have in our Secret World. Sometimes these roads are underdeveloped, made of gravel or dirt. They are not roads that we regularly travel, but they are the roads that have existed for the longest. These are typically thought processes that have been passed down from our families or have been developed by our past experiences. These are not the most popular roads in our cities, but these are the roads that we default to when all else has failed, when we are scared or hurting. These are what are referred to scientifically as cognitive biases. These roads are separated from rationality, and they are based on personally constructed reality. They are the back entrances of our cities. Cognitive biases may sometimes lead to a distorted perception of reality, an inaccurate judgment, or an illogical interpretation. These are the default settings and responses that have been built into us by our past circumstances and instructions. We try not to take these roads, but we fall back on them when we are exasperated or when it is our last resort. Taking these roads can get us lost quickly, and they can leave us feeling hopeless and stranded way out in the middle of nowhere.

These are the roads that cause many people to have racial biases and take on the belief of stereotypes. Even though racism is not something that most people ascribe to purposefully, many people have back roads that were blazed by their parents or their grandparents. This could have been accomplished through little remarks or jokes. You know, when we make light of something serious, it is usually an indication that there is a road that has been blazed that keeps us numb to empathy. I remember hearing my grandfather make snide remarks and comments when I was a child. He would make statements about people of this descent, and people of that descent, and even though I did not realize it at the time, the statements he made caused small roads to be traveled in my Secret World. The older I got, and the more experiences I had with people of all different cultures and ethnicities, the less these roads were traveled; however, they were still there, and whenever I would see a "this person" outside a store I would advise my wife to lock the doors while I ran inside. Whenever I would see a "that person," I would take my wallet out of my back pocket and clutch it a little tighter. These things might seem harmless enough, but they reveal some gravel roads that we have in our Secret Worlds. These biases are not just things that we easily overcome. Thoughts like these cannot be displaced they must be replaced! They do not go away on their own. They only go away through the renewal of the mind and a reception of the mind of Christ. Christ regards no race or ethnicity over another, He sees the value in every man and every woman.

These are also roads that cause us to have socioeconomic biases. When you see a homeless person on the side of the street, you think that they deserve to be there, or that they must be an addict instead of being moved with compassion like Jesus would have been. When someone at the checkout in front of you doesn't have enough money to pay for their groceries and they begin trying to decide what they need and what they have to put back and you immediately think they must just be a lazy person, if they can't provide for their family then they must not put in the work necessary. After all, we live in the land of opportunity, so if someone is not succeeding then it is on them. Instead, you should be realizing the blessings that you have, and that God is your provider, so your response should be to give, to help. I have been on both sides of this. I have been without a home, I have been without the money to afford groceries, and I have also been the person looking scornfully at the impoverished. These are thoughts that you aren't even aware that you hold, until you're confronted with them, these are the roads you hardly travel, but when you do, you see the degradation of your Secret World. These are just a few examples of some backroads I have personally had to destroy in my own soul.

    Another type of path that we travel in our cities are main roads. These are the simplest and least complicated of the three. They take us from one place to another. They are usually governed by reason and evidence. For most sane people, this is how our thoughts travel in a casual, everyday sense. They are the slowest type of road to travel because they usually consist of stop lights and stop signs, but the patience it takes to travel them also make them the most reliable of the three types listed, at least by natural standards. The most significant aspect of these roads is that they consist of many intersections. These intersections are where two separate thoughts converge. Our decisions can be made at the corner of family and hurt, perception and reality, or heartbreak and love. Although most think that they are mutually exclusive, faith can run right through doubt. As a matter of fact, many build monuments to religion right on the corner of faith and doubt. Our blended experiences can lead us to making decisions out of confusion.

    Our souls also consist of highways. Highways, in the natural, are the fastest means of getting around a city because they allow for a more direct path at a much higher speed. These highways that run through our brains are referred to as neural pathways. When brain cells communicate with great frequency, the bond between them is strengthened. This causes repeat thoughts, or patterns of thought, to transmit faster and faster. Physically, when we travel a road consistently, the journey becomes easier and easier. It becomes more natural to us.

This is exactly what happens in the minds of many believers. Through the repetition of thoughts, we get set into patterns of thought. These patterns cause our minds to automatically respond irrationally to certain stimuli. Sometimes we don't even understand why we are doing it. We don't know why a simple comment from a lady in line at the grocery store can cause us to respond so emotionally. We don't understand why we can get so angry and overwhelmed with frustration by a complete stranger in traffic. We don't get why our headache causes us to immediately assume we have a brain tumor. We don't understand why when a friend texts us a scripture, we immediately go into defense mode and think they are discounting our ability to hear from God. These things drive us crazy. They make us respond in a way that is completely irrational, but it is because we have created highways in our

Secret Worlds. We have given heed to thoughts and these roads are so well driven they happen naturally. One of the biggest threats to the church body is the lack of mind renewal.

> *Do not be conformed to this world, but be transformed by the renewal of your mind, that by testing you may discern what is the will of God, what is good and acceptable and perfect.*
>
> Romans 12:2, ESV

This verse emphasizes the essentiality of mind renewal for the people of God. The New International Version says, "do not conform to the pattern of this world." The pattern described is a pattern of thought. It is so easy for us to stay in our pre-Jesus patterns of thought because they are what have ruled us for the majority of our lives, but this is exactly why Jesus commissions us to lose our lives. In Second Corinthians Paul explains this mental attack in many instances. In chapter 4 verse 4 Paul exclaims that "the god of this world has blinded the minds of the unbelievers, to keep them from seeing the light of the gospel of the glory of Christ, who is the image of God" (ESV). In another instance, in chapter 11 verse 3 Paul says, "I am afraid that as the serpent deceived Eve by his cunning, your thoughts will be led astray from a sincere and pure devotion to Christ" (ESV). In chapter 2 verse 11, he states that we fight against the manipulation of our minds, so "that we would not be outwitted by Satan; for we are not ignorant of his designs" (ESV). In order for us to overcome the attack of the enemy and the patterns of thought we developed when we were citizens of this world system, every part of us has to die. This includes our old ways of thinking.

Neural pathways can become a really powerful tool for us as believers, and when developed properly, they can help us greatly in our walk in God. If we rewire our minds to turn to Jesus in every situation, if that is the singular highway that runs through our cityscape, then we are off to a great start dismantling the Secret World that has been established within us. This is the goal; however, this only comes through the establishment of a disciplined thought life.

whatever is true, whatever is honorable, whatever is just, whatever is pure, whatever is lovely, whatever is commendable, if there is any excellence, if there is anything worthy of praise, think about these things.

Philippians 4:8, ESV

Disciplining our thought life is controlling what we allow ourselves to think about. When we ponder on evil, we will inevitably become consumed by evil. When we ponder on Jesus and His perfection, then we will inevitably become more like Him. When you gaze at righteousness, purity is the only choice that remains.

CARNAL CONSTRUCTIONS

Now, understand that these roads, these patterns of thought, lead us somewhere. The highways and byways that our thoughts travel on lead us into the construction of architecture. They cause us to develop mindsets. When our thoughts continually travel to the same place over and over again, we develop buildings and monuments at those locations. This architecture can be dedicated to people, ideas, beliefs, or even things. They are created in honor of the objects and ideas that we give value to.

> *Those who are motivated by the flesh only pursue what benefits themselves. But those who live by the impulses of the Holy Spirit are motivated to pursue spiritual realities. For the mind-set of the flesh is death, but the mind-set controlled by the Spirit finds life and peace. In fact, the mind-set focused on the flesh fights God's plan and refuses to submit to his direction, because it cannot! For no matter how hard they try, God finds no pleasure with those who are controlled by the flesh.*
>
> Romans 8:5-8, TPT

Those who are motivated by the flesh are carnally minded. This means that they are body or sense ruled. They are governed by what is physical. For most people, extrinsic data is supreme authority. They are controlled by reality, or at the very least, the reality that the enemy presents them with. The carnal mind is hostile towards God. It produces death which is alienation from God. The world-city that is found in the soul is an enemy of God, and it will seek to oppose any colonization by the Holy Spirit. The enemy wants to build over the soil of divine real estate. He does this by taking your focus from God and getting you to be fleshly minded. You cannot have carnal mindsets and please God. You either oppose God or you oppose the world. There is no neutral ground.

As mentioned previously, carnal mindsets cause us to create architecture in our cities that opposes God. The most common type of architecture in our cities is the average run-of-the-mill building. Most cities are full of all kinds of buildings, some small and some massive. These buildings have various functions and they come to life at different times of day or night.

When we do things outside of the will of God, it opens the door for architecture to be built in our cities. When we sin, it allows us to create permanent structures that influence our cities' geography. Sin does not just include the things that the Bible points out specifically, but it also includes any form of disobedience to God. When we begin to compromise ourselves and fall back into our old nature, it makes us vulnerable to the hardening of our hearts. When we participate in the ways of the world, we become numb to the depravity of it. In Proverbs 8 verse 13 the scripture says that "the fear of the Lord is the hatred of evil" (ESV). When we fail to hate sin and evil, it is a pretty good indication that we have parts of it in us. We are called to be separate from the world, but when the ways of the world begin to become a part of us, we are no longer fulfilling this commission. When we continue to become desensitized towards wickedness, we become further disconnected from the heart of the Father, and this causes us to create an entire city that is irrespective of His plan for us.

Just like our natural cities are full of all types of buildings, the cities in our Secret Worlds are too. These buildings are erected through our emotions. The ways we respond emotionally to situations, materials, and people determines the type and size of the buildings that we create. In some instances, we disregard things altogether. These things tend to have no lasting impact on our cities. The things we disregard don't make a mark on us, but the things we regard change the geography of our Secret Worlds. When we love someone deeply, we create a whole structure that is dedicated to that love and that person. We might build a small building for our friends that we admire, and we might build another for our favorite movie. When we are angry and bitter towards a situation, we might create a massive structure that keeps bringing our attention back to the issue. Most of us have eyesores all over the place in our cities. We have hideous buildings that we have created in honor of negative emotions that we couldn't let go of. Some of us have buildings that are incomplete. We have buildings that we had begun building, but we gave up on because we were scared of what might happen, because we were scared of rejection. Some of our buildings are visited regularly, and some have been abandoned for years.

    This is all dependent on what we lend our emotions to. Our affections change the structure of our cities, and wherever they rest, we will find the largest structures. Please understand that emotions are not bad. Our emotions are gifts from God. They help us navigate and enjoy the world around us; however, our emotions are meant to serve us. God never intended for us to be ruled by them. They are to be submitted to The Father so that he can use them to better direct our steps. When they are not submitted to God, we run the risk of being controlled by them. When we are led by our emotions, structures are built. These emotions that were initially intended to serve us and strengthen our relationship with God are now obstructing it. They are creating architecture that interferes with our view of God.

Another type of architecture found in our cities is the monument. Monuments are built for the things or people that we have the highest esteem for. They are built for the things we worship, created through idolatry. Many people are under the misconception that idolatry is a practice of old. It is reserved for the pagans and those who revelled in Greek mythology. Our perception of idolatry is that it is the worship of a golden calf or a graven image. This is a form of idolatry, yes but this is not the typical idolatry we see in western cultures. The main form we deal with is elevating people, things, and beliefs above God. When we turn our gaze from The Father, it will eventually land on something or someone else. When our affection is not on The Father, it is only a matter of time until you replace His position with someone or something else. Idols demand worship, and, as beings created to worship, we are undoubtedly worshipping something. These modern idols are carved through emotional enchantments. They are slowly developed through our continued musings and dependencies on things outside of God. When we elevate a person, idea, or thing above God, it forces us to build massive structures of worship for them. Idols are especially dangerous because they will fight for their place when their idolatry is revealed by the light of the Holy Spirit. They will provide information, emotions, and evidence to keep their position on the throne of your heart.

What we must understand is that we serve a God who cares to have our attention and our affection. He wants connection with His people. This is why one of the earliest commandments in the bible is a warning against idolatry. In Exodus chapter 20 verses 4 through 5 it says, "You shall not make for yourself a carved image, or any likeness of anything that is in heaven above, or that is in the earth beneath, or that is in the water under the earth. You shall not bow down to them or serve them, for I the Lord your God am a jealous God..." (ESV). Our God is a jealous God. The word here used for *jealous* is the Hebrew word *qanna*. This word does not refer to the petty, immature jealousy we are familiar with. Rather, it refers to a demand for exclusive servitude. In western Christianity, we have built ideas about God that are incomplete. One of the ideas we have created is that we serve a God who asks nothing from us, but this is an incomplete revelation. In fact, God asks everything of us. He does not desire our abilities, our works, or our sacrifices; however, He adamantly demands our total surrender to Him. God asks us to submit our lives to His Lordship. HE IS A JEALOUS GOD, AND HE REFUSES TO SHARE OUR HEARTS. He desires, rather he demands, our exclusive servitude.

Apart from the monuments we build, we also create skyscrapers in our cities. Skyscrapers are erected in honor of unresolved bitterness that we carry. Bitterness causes us to resent people and God. When metal is put to metal, it becomes something so large that it reaches the heavens and obstructs your view of the light.

These things could be completely legitimate, or they could be complete nonsense; either way it matters not because the hurt is the same. We let that hurt seethe and boil until it becomes this massive structure in our Secret Worlds, until it becomes a skyscraper. Bitterness, just like skyscrapers, don't take up a lot of land, but they take up a lot of the cityscape. They don't possess wide bases, but they don't need to in order to have a significant impact on our perspectives. They are small things that we build up, higher and higher until they reach the heavens, until we can't go anywhere in our Secret Worlds without seeing them. It is the equivalent of seeing red when we are angry. We focus on it until we have bits of bitterness in the peripherals of our vision. Bitterness has the capacity to captivate anyone who will give it position. It will take control of your thought life, until it makes you into a person that is closed off and guarded, a person who refuses to trust.

In the book of Ruth, we see the story of Naomi, a woman who allowed her hurt to turn into bitterness. In the first chapter of this book, we meet Naomi and her family, who had to leave their homeland because of a famine. They look for refuge in Moab, and her sons eventually marry Moabite women. Not many years later, she loses her husband and both of her sons. With them all passing, Naomi is left with nothing other than her two daughters-in-law. Being a widow during this time was not easy, and without any sons to care for her, she was put in great danger. Naomi has no choice but to return home to try and seek refuge. In Ruth 1 verse 20 we get insight into Naomi's state of mind as she says, "... Don't call me Naomi. Call me Mara, she answered, for the Almighty has made me very bitter" (HCSB). The Hebrew word *Naomi* means pleasantness or happiness, while the Hebrew word *Mara* means bitterness. She let her pain lead her into bitterness, and then she began to identify with that bitterness. This is a dangerous place to be. It wrecked her and left her unable to process her pain. Thankfully for Naomi, she had a daughter-in-law, Ruth, that surrendered herself to God as a tool to knock down the architecture that bitterness was trying to build, but had she stayed there, it would have led to the construction of a skyscraper that would have altered her view of God.

Further, we have memorials that we build in our cities. Memorials are structures that we create in our cities in honor of things or people we have lost. The intention is that they serve as focal points that bring back memories. These memorials can come in the shape of a landmark, a fountain, a museum, or a work of art. Regardless of the type of memorial built, these become epicenters of sobering pain. People build memorials so they will remember what and who they've lost. They carve names onto the side of the walls. They place flowers on the doors, and when the time rolls around, they mourn. We take people to the memorials in our cities, and we show them the things we have lost, like their memory serves to excuse our actions and our inability to maintain control.

We use these memorials as a way to cope with overwhelming grief; however, they are only temporary fixes that do not provide any true healing. God cares for us, and he doesn't want us to remain in these places of pain. He wants us to release our grief to Him, so that he can heal our brokenness and restore us to joy.

> *He heals the wounds of every shattered heart. He sets his stars in place, calling them all by their names. How great is our God! There's absolutely nothing his power cannot accomplish, and he has infinite understanding of everything.*
>
> Psalm 147:3-5, TPT

The Lord who has designed all of creation, The God who is able to accomplish more than we could ever ask or need, is the same God who wants to reach into your hurt. He is the same God that wants to heal your hurt. All of the architecture that you build in your Secret World is about keeping you from His healing power. It is all built as a tactic to obstruct your view of God by causing you to develop a crowded cityscape.

The Secret World, the world that talks to you when no one is around, the world that you are always interacting with, is filled with all of this architecture that causes our view of God and His divine truth to be obstructed. And even though you look good on the outside, you could be in turmoil on the inside. It may be sunny and 72 degrees on the outside, but you've got storms on the inside. The enemy comes in to seize control of your city, and he breaches the walls at strategic places. He gets in and works to convince you into a great exchange, the Secret Place for the Secret World. The devil loves that because he can get you to fantasize and think about things and build things in your head. These things might give temporary relief, but they will not solve the problems. The Secret Place is the only place where problems are solved, not the Secret World. The more the enemy can build inside of your city, the more difficult it is to dismantle. He is constantly at work, but what Jesus did out works every attempt he makes.

Many people say that only time heals deep-seated wounds, but that is not true in any regard. Time doesn't do much to heal our minds, only renewal and deconstruction does.

Once we recognize the architecture in our cities, the only thing left is deconstruction. This is a very difficult and painful process because, although the Holy Spirit is a gentle comforter, He is also a mighty wrecking ball. He fervently desires us to see the beauty of Jesus Christ, and that beauty is clouded by everything that is contrary to Him.

CITY CULTURE

In order for any city to be successful it has to have its own unique culture. This is the term used to describe the social behaviors and norms for a society. A culture enables a free flow of ideas and exchange. A city's culture is what attracts us to it. It is what makes it different from others. A lot of variables go into the construction of the culture of our Secret Worlds. Our culture is primarily built through experiences, beliefs, and preferences. Each successful city has what are called city sectors or districts. For example, we all have an entertainment sector and an arts district. We have a manufacturing center as well as a shipping and receiving sector. We've got a financial district, an education district, and a religious district. With all of these intricacies in mind, our cities are absolutely booming. There are all kinds of different things that are going on within the city, all kinds of things that are going on within us.

In our various sectors, decisions are being finalized. In our financial district, we are deciding where to spend our money. We are determining what holds value. When our financial district is overrun by our entertainment district, we tend to waste money on frivolous and fleeting things. Most people have a hard time giving because they have placed every other city sector in between their finances and the church, completely unaware that their financial district would be blessed and enhanced by giving to the church. Some people have placed their religious district right next to their educational district, and this keeps them from understanding God spiritually. They can only understand Him intellectually. They lack intimacy and any true connection because they have to reason all of the miraculous and supernatural elements of scripture away.

The placement of these sectors, and how well they are developed, manipulates the way we respond to external stimuli just like our thought patterns do. In essence, the cultures of our cities rule over our responses to the outside world. Now, if you study physical cities, you'll realize the physical cities have characteristics to them and personalities all based upon the people that live in them and the districts that have received more attention. The biggest city that is close to my home is Tulsa. Tulsa is best known for its art district. It is also often referred to as the city of murals because many of the buildings have colorful expressions of art canvasing the outside walls. It also has many galleries and exhibits. This has become a huge part of the culture of Tulsa. Because the art district has been emphasized so heavily, things that are associated with people who enjoy art are also emphasized. For example, there are many wine bars and coffee shops in Tulsa because when one goes to examine art, they often stop by one or the other. These elements make Tulsa attractive for many young artists and relevant hipsters. They are drawn to the culture of the city.

The city that I actually live in is a very small city, and the primary district is our education district. The whole city is built to serve the school. Due to this, our city's entertainment, art, and finances are all wrapped up in the school. If we want to enjoy a show, we attend the high school performance of *Into the Woods*. If we want to be entertained, we attend a high school football game. Our singular grocery store donates regularly to our students. Our churches have programs that are built specifically for the students in our town. The culture of our city is founded on our education district because it is the area that has been given the most emphasis. It is the aspect of the city that is most valued by its inhabitants. Due to this, many families with children are drawn to it. They are attracted to a city that emphasizes the next generation.

Likewise, the city that inhabits your Secret World has its very own unique culture. This culture has been created by the district, or districts, that you have given the most weight to. You and I could live right next door to each other and internally exist within completely different cultures. Some people regard education above all else. These people are usually prideful, and they elevate their minds above the word of God. They value intellect, and they value people who have higher education. They hold onto their honor and only distribute it out when someone has met their standard of intelligence. They have degrees that they cling to, and they are the source of their pride and success. Some people regard entertainment above all else. These people are usually glutenous and lascivious. They have no regard for reasonability; they solely want to satisfy their desires. The satisfaction of these desires hold preeminence in their lives. They will spend their money on concerts, alcohol, food, and clubs. Others regard family above all else. These people are usually idolatrous. They worship their children and can't wait to tell everyone about what grade they got on their spelling test or how their children are so much better than all of the others because they learned to write at the age of 48 months. They miss church regularly for their children's sporting events, and they feel justified in doing so because they think they are being good parents in doing this. They are loyal to a fault, and they will argue with their child's teacher to get them an extra point on their homework because, in their eyes, their family can do no wrong. Whatever category you fit into, or if you fit into an internal culture category that isn't even listed here, it is all wrong. ANY CULTURE CONTRARY TO KINGDOM CULTURE IS ANTI CHRIST.

Now, I understand that this is a hard pill to swallow, and this struck a tender chord for many of you who are reading; however, this is Truth. There are many challenges that the Spirit of God has to overcome in us to cancel the enemies' advances. The Holy Spirit wants to integrate us into the culture of the Kingdom, but this integration is difficult because the enemy develops divisions in the body of Christ through beliefs, facts, preferences, and ideologies. Many times, our internal culture is in conflict with the culture of the Kingdom. This creates many obstacles to achieving Kingdom objectives in the soul.

> *Do not love the world or the things in the world. If anyone loves the world, the love of the Father is not in him. For all that is in the world—the desires of the flesh and the desires of the eyes and pride of life—is not from the Father but is from the world. And the*

world is passing away along with its desires, but whoever does the will of God abides forever.

1 John 2:15-17, ESV

If your desire, your mindset, or your focus is outside of Jesus, then you are in the wrong. Many believers get so caught up in the world that the world becomes a part of them. They develop a culture that is contrary to the father and begin to desire the things of the world. We as believers need to become inundated with the culture of the Kingdom. There needs to be no differentiation between what we are experiencing on the inside of us and what is being experienced in Heaven. The goal is not just for your internal culture to be flipped upside down, but for the culture of the world to be as well. This can only occur through the working out of our salvation.

FORTIFYING YOUR CITY

In the previous section we discussed the sectors that are in our cities. We considered how the development of these sectors can lead to the creation of an internal culture, an expression of man and Satan that can cause his agenda to be manifested through our lives rather than the will of God. The moment that you become aware of these things; the enemy begins to tighten his grip. You might have already felt that since you've begun reading this book. It is possible that you have already felt yourself fall under attack. You might feel offense creeping in, or you might feel bitterness towards me or someone else. These responses are very natural for both believers and unbelievers alike because revelation will always be met with opposition. This opposition happens so rapidly because the enemy has built strongholds within your city. A stronghold is a place in your Secret World that acts as a hiding spot for ideas and beliefs. It is a place where the enemy is protected and hidden from our awareness. The enemy breaks in and sets up strongholds and traps that keep you held captive. Let's look at the book of Proverbs.

A man without self-control is like a city broken into and left without walls.

Proverbs 25:28, ESV

Here we have a very interesting analogy brought by the Holy Spirit through Solomon. When someone cannot control their anger, or restrain themselves emotionally, they are like a city that has been taken over. The walls of protection have been broken down. Now, how many have ever run into somebody, and you recognize right off the bat that they are without restraint. They say everything that comes in their head. They don't care about the cost. They cannot restrain their emotions. They are completely overrun by their feelings. One day they're happy, and the next they're in the absolute pits. They don't have any consistency in their life. It's because their city has been taken over. I can guarantee that you have someone in mind right now, it might even be yourself. That's okay, as they say, the first step to overcoming a problem is admitting that you have a problem.

We know the enemy uses loss and hurts as an opportunity to penetrate the walls of your heart. When you are vulnerable, the enemy uses it as an opportunity to break into your city. Once inside your breached city, he begins to build things inside of you. He begins to build strongholds. That is the purpose of all of the buildings he gets you to erect. He covers and protects himself inside the walls of your city. He creates a place for himself inside your Secret World, a place that is not easily revoked, a place that is hidden behind closed doors. He hides himself and his cowardly minions inside those buildings, monuments, and skyscrapers. In those buildings, he creates erroneous ideas about the Bible, inaccurate interpretations of God's person, and distorted perspectives about the way that God sees us. Layer by layer he builds lies into the foundation and architecture of our cities. Through these lies, he begins to soften our perspective towards sin, until we are no longer convicted by it.

For example, a young girl who had been sexually abused and her parents didn't find out about this abuse until much later. She was too afraid to tell them the truth because she felt like somehow it was her fault. This is, unfortunately, a situation that many people find themselves in. The shame and hurt eating away at them. The enemy uses this hurt as a means to break into her Secret World. She allows monuments and buildings to be assembled in her city. She begins to develop a mistrust for all men. This mistrust eventually turns into a hatred that prevents her from honoring and respecting men. Now, anytime a man gets close to her the enemy reminds her of her past hurt. Her pain becomes fresh again, and she guards herself. She feels the pain of the past rising up in her again, so she just refuses to let her walls down. Not only does this damage her physical relationships, but when Jesus tries to draw near to her, the enemy tightens his grips and whispers lies. He convinces her that Jesus will just hurt her and control her just like her grandfather did. He manipulates her into believing that Jesus is like all of the other men. He validates his own existence through refusing Christ's access into her soul realm.

Another example, a businessman gets messed over on a deal he made with a close friend. He loses a great deal of his finances in this investment gone wrong. He also develops skepticism and lack of trust in his friendships. The enemy uses this disappointment as a way to breach his city. The enemy leaps the wall that the disappointment left damaged and fallen. Now the man plays his hand close to his chest. He refuses to take any financial risks that could leave him in that vulnerable state again. He refuses to trust those closest to him. He has a firm grip on his money, and anytime someone compels him to give, something on the inside becomes immediately defensive. He has to protect what he has, and no one or nothing, especially not the church, is going to get his money. His inability to give and take financial risks limits his ability to make progress. It hinders his ability to experience breakthrough. His inability to be vulnerable in his relationships leaves him feeling lonely and unfulfilled.

Now, these are just a few examples of how the enemy does this in our lives, but the idea is the same. When we experience loss or hurt, we are left in a vulnerable position. Our walls are broken down, and we become susceptible to the enemy's attacks. He uses these hurts as opportunities to breach our cities, to climb the broken-down walls. Once he is inside his agenda is initiated. He uses all of the formerly mentioned tools to build and create structures in your life. He creates highways, buildings, skyscrapers, monuments, memorials, sectors, and cultures. These things are not created in vain. They are created to protect him and his legion. They are specifically designed as strongholds that give the enemy a stake in your life. These strongholds exist inside of all of us, and they are pockets of protection for the enemy to exist within. They are hideouts for his gangs.

> *...our gospel is veiled, it is veiled to those who are perishing. The god of this age has blinded the minds of unbelievers, so that they cannot see the light of the gospel that displays the glory of Christ, who is the image of God.*
>
> 2 Corinthians 4:3-4, NIV

The enemy, the god of this age, has worked to blind the minds of unbelievers through their partnership with sin. He also works to blind the minds of believers in the same way. The word used here for veiled is the Greek word *Kaluptó*. This word means to cover up, to keep secret, to hide as if in a hut or cabin. He blinds us through the creation of strongholds that veil us from seeing the light of the gospel.

One thing most Christians do not understand is that we are in a war for our souls. There is a daily battle for control in our soul realm. The Lord, the commander of

Heaven's armies, and the spiritual entities that are in rebellion against God are both in a battle for the throne room of your heart. The enemy is outnumbered, outpowered, and stripped of all the authority that he once had, so his only option is a strategic war. Thinking back to the American Revolutionary war, this was very much the case with the American patriots. They were outnumbered, outpowered, and they had no authority backing them. The one thing they did have, however, was the home court advantage. The patriots had a thorough knowledge of the terrain and how to use it against their British colonizers. There is one famous battle in particular where we see this advantage prove invaluable. That is at the famous Battle of Bunker Hill. The American patriots set themselves at the top of Bunker Hill, and they used their geographical position as a stronghold of defense against the British. Even though they didn't naturally have the ability to stand against the British army, their positioning gave them an advantage. Because they held the high ground, the British could not clearly see their enemy. The patriots were given the ability to sparingly use their limited supply of ammunition by waiting until they saw the whites of the British soldier's eyes before they fired. The British went up in 3 different waves and were forced back down the hill in a retreat after the first two, losing many soldiers. Even though the Americans eventually lost this battle, they killed and incapacitated a major portion of the British Army. This changed the tide of the Revolutionary war and severely crippled the British.

What is the point of this mini history lesson? I want you to see that a strategically placed stronghold can cripple your ability to achieve the freedom Christ purchased for you. The enemy uses strategically placed architecture in your Secret Worlds as geographical strongholds in order to acquire the advantage. He wants to validate his place in your life. He wants to incapacitate you and keep you from God. He doesn't just want to help you build this city, he wants to control it, so he has entities that seek through Trojan horses, to breach the walls of your mind and begin to set up residencies inside your city.

Say, for instance, that the enemy wants to keep you broke, keep you in a poverty mindset. He will seek to establish strongholds, thoughts, and ideas within the financial sector of your city; however, he doesn't stop there because he knows, without fortification, you might find out something that would break you out of that poverty mindset. He seeks to bring inhabitants into your city to reinforce your predisposed ideas and notions. They begin to control and dominate, and when revelation light comes to us, there's a rage in the streets. There's a riot, and all the information that you've built up, these entities come to enforce. They try to talk to you and to dissuade you from obedience.

In order to do this, he must strengthen and reinforce the places he creates. Subsequently, he doesn't just build strongholds in your Secret World, but he also works tirelessly to fortify these strongholds.

There are many things that can lead to the fortification of strongholds in your life. The examples above are meant to show real life events that can compromise your city walls, but, once your walls are compromised and the enemy is inside your city walls, what is it that causes strongholds to be fortified? There are many things that can cause the fortification of strongholds, and to create an exhaustive list would take a great deal of time, but for our purposes, I will list a few of the most common things that lead to the fortification of strongholds in our inner worlds. As a pastor, these are the things that I see most frequently, the things that plague the people of God. The first being secret sin.

The fact of the matter is that what Jesus did on the cross led to our victory over all sin. In that moment, the power of sin and death was overcome once and for all. Many people receive their freedom and then willingly submit themselves again to the yoke of slavery. In Galatians chapter 5 verse number 1, Paul says, "For freedom Christ has set us free; stand firm therefore, and do not submit again to a yoke of slavery" (ESV). If we are free, why do we have to stand firm? Because if we do not, we submit ourselves again to the slavery of sin. The freedom that Christ purchased for us is in our possession, but in order for us to live from that freedom, we must stand firm. The word used here for stand firm is the Greek word *stékó,* which means to walk in holiness, to live in the fear of God. Sin in itself, however, is not what causes strongholds to be rectified and fortified in our soul realms. Perpetual sin does separate us from God, not because it moves Him but because it moves us. The cause of fortification is not sin in and of itself. The cause is hidden sin. The things that you deal with in secret, in darkness, are the things that the enemy uses to fortify the strongholds he is building. What is in the light, will be overcome by the light; however, what is in the shadows is hidden from the light. Now, I understand that nothing is really hidden from the Spirit of God that searches our hearts, but when we keep things tucked away in darkness, the light of the Father's love cannot shine on it. The enemy thrives on secrecy. Secrecy leads to shame, isolation, and condemnation. When we find ourselves under the sway of these enemies to the cross, we are unable to connect to the father. When we are unable to connect to the Father, the enemy has greater access to our soul realm because we find ourselves under the compulsion of sin.

How do we destroy the strongholds that are built and strengthened through our hidden sins? We do this through confession. We bring the sin into the light. Now, hear me. I am not saying to shout your indiscretions from the rooftops. I do not believe we should be careless in this way. Not everyone has your best interest at heart and confession to the wrong person could lead to hurt and ruin, but still James tells us to confess.

> *Therefore, confess your sins to one another and pray for one another, that you may be healed. The prayer of a righteous person has great power as it is working.*
>
> James 5:16, ESV

The call here is to confess your sins to your mature brothers and sisters in Christ, those who walk in righteousness. It is established here that your confession will lead to healing because the prayer of the righteous has great power. We are called into repentance and when we repent, when we turn from our wicked ways, God promises restoration.

If we [freely] admit that we have sinned and confess our sins, He is faithful and just [true to His own nature and promises], and will forgive our sins and cleanse us continually from all unrighteousness [our wrongdoing, everything not in conformity with His will and purpose].

1 John 1:9, AMP

We can have confidence that when we bring things into the light we will not be met with shame and condemnation. The Lord will not come to us in anger and spite, but He will love us into freedom and healing. He will shine his glorious light on us and empower us to live in freedom.

Another thing that fortifies strongholds in our Secret Worlds is unforgiveness. Unforgiveness is the quickest way to surrender the mastery of your emotions to the enemy. It leads to bitterness, and bitterness that is harbored has a great deal of adverse effects on the body. The enemy will use his dominance over your emotions to keep you in bondage, to keep you from the freedom that Christ purchased for you. He will use your unforgiveness to keep your mind occupied and off of the Kingdom. Not only does this lead to spiritual and mental bondage, but it can also cause physical harm to your body. Karen Swartz, a doctor at John Hopkins, has dedicated a great deal of her time to researching the effects that unforgiveness and bitterness can have on the physical body. Her research concludes that it can lead to bad cholesterol, high blood pressure, sleep apnea, and a weakened immune system (Swartz). Holding onto this bitterness is detrimental to your overall health, so what are we to do about this type of stronghold?

You probably guessed it! We are to offer forgiveness, freely and regularly. This is essential for our health. Forgiving others releases the stress that causes strain on our hearts and immune systems. Studies show that people who refuse to hold grudges possess more energy, a better immune system, and a healthier heart. This is reason enough to make forgiveness a part of your daily lives, but it also connects us more directly to the heart of the Father. There is a passage in Matthew that warns of the danger of unforgiveness.

> Then Peter came up and said to him, "Lord, how often will my brother sin against me, and I forgive him? As many as seven times?" Jesus said to him, "I do not say to you seven times, but seventy-seven times. Therefore, the kingdom of heaven may be compared to a king who wished to settle accounts with his servants. When he began to settle, one was brought to him who owed him ten thousand talents. And since he could not pay, his master ordered him to be sold, with his wife and children and all that he had, and payment to be made. So, the servant fell on his knees, imploring him, 'Have patience with me, and I will pay you everything.' And out of pity for him, the master of that servant released him and forgave him the debt. But when that same servant went out, he found one of his fellow servants who owed him a hundred denarii, and seizing him, he began to choke him, saying, 'Pay what you owe.' So his fellow servant

fell down and pleaded with him, 'Have patience with me, and I will pay you.' He refused and went and put him in prison until he should pay the debt. When his fellow servants saw what had taken place, they were greatly distressed, and they went and reported to their master all that had taken place. Then his master summoned him and said to him, 'You wicked servant! I forgave you all that debt because you pleaded with me. And should not you have had mercy on your fellow servant, as I had mercy on you?' And in anger his master delivered him to the jailers, until he should pay all his debt. So also my heavenly Father will do to every one of you, if you do not forgive your brother from your heart."

Matthew 18:21-35, ESV

This passage is a humbling reminder of how we should respond to the mercy of God. Jesus gives one of the greatest parables in the gospels about this man that was forgiven of an insurmountable debt. His master releases him to his freedom by canceling the debt, which is a type and shadow of Jesus' work on the cross for us. The man gets out on the street, and he sees another man that happens to owe him fifty dollars. He puts this guy in a headlock, takes him to the magistrate, and has him thrown into prison. See, Jesus tells us that if we've been forgiven, then we need to forgive. Ephesians 5, 1 says, "Be imitators of God, as dear children" (NKJ). Notice what Jesus says, Jesus wasn't angry with the person who owed the fifty dollars. Jesus was upset with the person who wouldn't forgive because he had been forgiven of such a great debt. He says he will be delivered to the tormentors. What does He mean? He means that unforgiveness opens the door for demonic spirits. When we see demonically oppressed people, we must understand that they have gone through a process. Their walls have been broken down through some sort of hurt or pain, and the enemy has been able to infiltrate, build structures, and fortify those structures.

Many see this passage, and they are immediately taken back by how this man responds. They are astonished that he would have the audacity to refrain from giving mercy when he had been forgiven such a massive debt; however, this is what it looks like to God when we refuse to forgive those who trespass against us. We are no different than the man who is presented in this story. We often see ourselves as better because we compare our successes to other people's failures, but we have all sinned and fallen short of the glory of God (Romans 3:23). We have turned from God over and over again. We chose sin when He was an option. We chose our own way when He had a perfect destiny set before us. We chose temporary satisfaction over the eternal goodness that The Creator has prepared for us, and yet God still chose to forgive us. Jesus still chose to sacrifice himself on our behalf. It is astonishing to think we would ever have the right to hold a grudge against someone else. I don't say any of this to bring condemnation. This is something I have to continually remind myself of, but when we choose to follow Christ, we must follow His mercy as well. We must humble ourselves and remember that to refuse to forgive is to refuse to be like Jesus.

Finally, strongholds are fortified through lies that you have given your faith to. Did you know that you put faith behind everything you believe? We all live by faith. When we give our faith to a lie, we lend one of our greatest giftings to that lie. The reason why people are so confused, the reason why the world is in such turmoil, is because too many believers have lent their faith to lies. We have listened to lies about God, and many Christians have been the ones to spread lies about God. Many pastors and teachers spread lies about God from the very pulpit that God gave them. We listen to lies about ourselves. We convince ourselves that we are not enough. We convince ourselves of our wretchedness and our inability to live righteous lives, our inability to overcome sin. We believe lies about how God sees us. We believe that sometimes He chooses to refuse our healing. We believe that He gets mad at us. We buy into the lies that the enemy has been playing over and over in our mind for years. In our pain, we allow these things in, we accept them as truth, and they fortify the places we've built to house the enemy.

How are we to fight these lies? We are meant to refute the lies with the truth! If anything in our lives does not stand up against the scrutiny of the Word of God, then we must be willing to surrender it freely. We surrender through a process of meditation and confession. We turn our musings towards the things of God and away from the lies. We confess the word over our lives. In many cases, lies can be easier to believe than the truth. This is because lies from the enemy can be backed by physical evidence. They can be reinforced by symptoms in your body, the words of a friend, or even a diagnosis from a doctor. The thing we must realize is that facts don't always lend themselves to the truth. This is something that may be confusing. It is a difficult concept to wrap our minds around in the natural. As Christians, we have been given a sixth sense called faith. This sense is the most powerful because it gives us the ability to tap into truth when all else points to the lie. Faith in God's Word gives us the ability to counteract the lie. Even when we cannot experience the truth with our physical senses, it gives us the ability to experience it through the word of God.

Each of the previously mentioned things works to fortify the strongholds of the enemy. This is why it is absolutely essential for us to stand firm and guard ourselves against these things. When we are not actively fighting against these things, we are passively absorbing them. There is no neutral ground for a believer. We are either progressing towards the heart of the father, or our stagnation is causing us to digress back into our humanity.

Furthermore, it is essential that we address the issues that lead us into the fortification of the strongholds the enemy intends to build. We will inevitably face disappointment, hurt, and temptation. There will be times where we find ourselves vulnerable, and where the enemy finds weak points in our walls, but when he attacks, we do not have to lend him our power. It is time for the church to fortify themselves. It is time for all of us to fortify our cities, to seek God and give Him full permission to search out and destroy every stronghold that the enemy has established in our Secret Worlds. He desires for us to be whole, but He only has access to what we give Him access to.

How do we do this? How do we undo the advances of the enemy? How do we reveal his hiding places? The answer is really simple: we find a new stronghold, and we hide ourselves in it. In Psalm chapter 18 verse 2 it says, "The LORD is my rock and my fortress and my deliverer, my God, my rock, in whom I take refuge, my shield, and the horn of my salvation, my stronghold" (ESV). When the enemy comes in and fortifies the strongholds that he helped create, he intends to protect himself and other spirits against their removal. He wants to defend beliefs and opinions that he established in you. He wants to validate his right to exist in your Secret World. So, we must fortify ourselves under the shadow of God's mighty hand. We must hide ourselves in His love because He is our salvation and our stronghold! He protects us against the advances of the enemy. He built a tower for us out of cedar boards before we were established on the earth (Song of Songs 8:9, TPT). In Psalm 27 verse 1 it says "The Lord is my light and my salvation; whom shall I fear? The Lord is the stronghold of my life; of whom shall I be afraid?" (ESV). The enemy can come. He can try to build and hide and destroy, but we have A GOD who established our redemption from the beginning of creation. He is the stronghold of our lives, and in Him all other strongholds are demolished.

As we have discussed, the spirit and the soul comprise what the Bible calls the heart. The heart has four chambers, we can see this physically. Well, the spiritual heart has four chambers as well-your spirit, your mind, your will, and your emotions. When we are wholehearted, we release the kingdom of God into our natural realm. When we have a divided heart, then it is absolutely neutralized. Our desire and goal should be to destroy cosmopolis, not just for ourselves, but for others as well. There are many ways the enemy seeks to neutralize the power of God in our lives, He seeks to build cosmopolis in us and through us.

We have looked at the roads that run through our cities, the backroads and the main streets. We have looked at how our thought patterns create neural pathways that act as the highways and byways in our cities and how these neural pathways must be retrained so that Jesus is our immediate response in time of trouble. We have examined our city sectors and how these sectors lend themselves to an internal culture when they are emphasized. We know that when our internal culture is contrary to the culture of the Kingdom, it causes us to respond in a way that is devoid of Christ's love and power. It is apparent that the enemy is looking to drive a wedge between us and God, and all of these aspects of our Secret World are tools he uses to accomplish this task. We understand that separation is what the enemy seeks to do. This separation is a part of his ultimate agenda, to develop a world that is contrary to God, a world that is Anti-Christ, however, if he wants to maintain control of this world, he cannot do it on his own. He needs to fill your city with inhabitants, inhabitants that can help him keep you in bondage.

Section 3:
Taking Capitol Hill

There are rural and underdeveloped areas of your soul realm. These areas consist of memories long since forgotten. These might be moments that rarely have relevance in your life. They have a place in your Secret World, but they don't have much influence. The rural areas might be occupied by those family members that you saw at gatherings as a child. They might contain an old friend or two, but for the most part, these portions of your Secret World are pretty desolate. They don't have a whole lot of traffic or bustle to them. The portion of your Secret World that is the most concentrated is found at the center. This is the area that directly surrounds the throne of your heart. Depending on who occupies the throne of your heart, this can look very different. If you are on the throne of your heart, then the city surrounds the throne.

Every Secret World has its own capitol. The city that the enemy helps you build is complete with its very own capitol district. This is the central aspect of your Secret World. When God is on the throne, then nature surrounds the throne. His love perpetuates the organic. But if you are on the throne, then concrete surrounds it. The center of your city becomes the epicenter for pride and offence.

UNRESTRAINED URBANIZATION

I remember back in the summer of 1990 my wife, Karen, and I were doing door to door evangelism. We would walk the streets of our local town and knock on each door. Street by street and house by house we would canvas for Jesus. It seemed like the majority of people were outside, or their doors were open if they were inside. Back then, you could look right through the screen door, or the glass door and people would welcome you right in. A lot has changed since then, but we noticed a drastic change the very next summer we went out to do the same type of evangelism and everything was completely different.

Same season, same weather, same everything, but every door was shut. No one was outside, and most people didn't even answer the door when we knocked. We could hear the people inside. We could hear their televisions, so we knew someone was in there, but they didn't respond. What changed? What was different between those two summers? In 1991, the world wide web was made accessible to the public, and everyone was inside searching and browsing. A couple of years later the enemy brought in high-speed internet. We started with that godforsaken Dial Up. I don't know if you remember that, but it was torturous.

The sound of the AOL Dial Up still haunts me in my sleep. Anyway, in the early 2000's, Dial Up got replaced, and we all began to get access to high-speed browsing, and again another wave of disconnection came. People began to become consumed by the internet, and by their own Secret World.

I don't want you to get the wrong idea, the internet and the advancement of technology is not innately wrong. There are many wonderful things that we have been given because of these advancements. Many people who did not previously have access to the word of God now had access. Many people now have access to sermons and sermon archives that they would have otherwise never been able to hear. We can broadcast and share the gospel with people all over the world because of these advancements, but many bad things came with it as well. You see, the danger of the internet is that it introduces things at a very rapid pace to your Secret World.

The enemy wants to create cosmopolis, so how is he going to do that? He is going to manipulate something God ordained for his own benefit. He is going to introduce information to the masses at a rapid pace, so he can begin to control our minds and inevitably the global narrative. He begins getting everyone to look at a screen, and then technology advances to a place where that screen can be carried with you everywhere you go. Now, he has a tool that is in the hands of most individuals. You used to have to wait until you got off work to go do your little sneaky stuff on the computer, but now you can just do it right there while you're at your job. Even the homeless population has been given access to phones in recent years. Almost everywhere you go has free WIFI that you can access, and it is rarer now than ever for people to not have access to the internet.

He is rapidly infiltrating your Secret Worlds with arguments, opinions, and thoughts. He is constantly flooding your soul with things that manipulate and build on the inside of you. Urbanization refers to a shift in the population and concentration of an area towards the city. This is exactly what the enemy wants to do in your Secret Worlds, he wants to build things that snuff out nature because he wants to obscure your view of God. He wants you to get so focused on the city that God doesn't matter. The internet and technology have been massive tools by which he has done this.

He doesn't want you to know what you were born to do. He doesn't want you to know the calling that's on your life. He doesn't want you to know the books that were written about you before you were even born. He doesn't want you to have any of that information whatsoever, so he distracts you. All of a sudden, every time that you get down on your knees to pray and begin to seek the Lord, the city starts reeling. You hear voices and complaints flooding you. "You need to get up, your knees hurt. You don't need to be doing that, you could be doing something else. You could be listening to music, or there's some stuff on TV that would be really entertaining." You hear all of these things when you are seeking the Lord because that is where you discover what you were created to do. When you enter into prayer, you open the gates to the Secret Place. You access it, and that is where the secrets are divulged, that is where the mysteries are explained. The enemy despises that, so when you begin to seek the Lord, your phone goes off. You get text after text, absolutely ludicrous, stupid stuff, but you feel that you have to give attention to it because you're more partial to your city than you are to what God is saying to you. You are more interested in the tour of your city that is flashing by, and it is causing rapid and unrestrained urbanization in your Secret World. This whole process is leading to the reaffirming of your capitol hill. It is drawing people and spirits into your city center. The larger and more developed your city center, the more fortified that your offences and your pride are.

EMBASSY OF OFFENSE

If you were to visit our nation's capital, Washington, D.C. you would see the National Library, the Lincoln Memorial, the White House, and many other historically significant places. One thing that you may find very fascinating is the neighborhood that holds the international embassies. In D.C. there is an entire district just outside of Capitol Hill that houses ambassadors from other nations all over the world. Their embassies are safe places that signify a plot of land that has a completely different set of laws. They represent foreign soil right in the middle of our nation. This is what offence does in our hearts. Even though we are citizens of the kingdom of heaven, when we allow offence to come in, it establishes embassies. It makes room for the enemy to create a plot of land in our hearts that has its own set of rules and freedoms.

Offence can be caused by a plethora of things. It could be caused by a message we heard a pastor preach that we felt was "directed straight at us," or a statement that was made that we felt was intended to cut us down. It could have nothing to do with church or God at all. Potentially, it was a friend who made you feel inadequate or talked down to you. You begin to seep in that moment and to give it weight until it grows into something huge. The enemy whispers probabilities in our ears in hopes of convincing us of what the people who hurt us meant. Did you know that the enemy will present you with whatever information is necessary to keep you separated from God? He will provide false evidence and use your imagination to convince you of all kinds of deceits.

In Matthew 5 verse 29 through 30

And if thy right eye offend thee, pluck it out, and cast it from thee: for it is profitable for thee that one of thy members should perish, and not that thy whole body should be cast into hell. And if thy right hand offend thee, cut it off, and cast it from thee: for it is profitable for thee that one of thy members should perish, and not that thy whole body should be cast into hell (KJV).

What are we to do with offence? We are called to pluck it out, to cast it from us. When we are presented with offence, we must rid ourselves of it as quickly and completely as possible. Offence that is not dealt with works to destroy us completely. It gives the enemy possession of land in our cities. We have no choice but to release it, or our soul finds itself in peril.

DISMANTLING THE CITADEL OF PRIDE

At the center of your city there is a citadel defended by fanatics. This citadel was constructed by your own ego. It was built by your personal desires and dreams. It is a place that is solely about you. It is completely selfish, and it is sitting in the middle of your city. It is a big edifice called pride. This is the central aspect of your city because pride builds the city.

Pride in its simplest form is uninvolvement with God. This means that there is an entire section of your life that's totally uninvolved with God. You might be involved in some areas with God. In some areas you might give Him minimal control, but in other areas of your city, there is absolutely no involvement, and it shows. If you go to the nearest city to you, you will quickly notice that there are many different sectors. Each of these sectors have varying degrees of positive involvement. You can see where law and order rules and where law and order does not. In most cities, the lawless sections are growing at a far more rapid pace, and this is true for those sections in our Secret Worlds as well. When we don't allow the Word of God to become the governing factor, lawlessness prevails.

God wants to restore us. He wants to restore the original inside-out reality of life. You were created to live life from the inside out. Sin causes us to live life from the outside in. The outside tells us who we are. We don't get picked for the softball team, and the outside tells us we're a failure. When we don't get the promotion at work, the outside tells us that we are not adequate. We were never meant to live from the outside. That is not how we were designed to operate. We can't live by our successes and failures on the outside because they will manipulate us. This is the reason why the bible tells you to guard yourself against not just criticism, but also praise. If you want to be a balanced human being, you need to know how to take criticism, and you need to know how to take praise because some people will go crazy when you praise them. They run with it and think they are going to be the next famous pastor or musician. Sometimes people just say things to be polite: "Oh you did a good job. Yeah, that was pretty good." They're just trying to be nice because they know people won't hang around if they say everything that they think, but some people take a polite compliment and let it inflate their egos to an unbearable size. We have to learn how to take both criticism and praise with humility, so that we don't attract more stuff into our Secret Worlds.

Pride draws in everything that's nefarious in your city. It has absolutely no regard for the things of God, for the words of God. Pride attracts inhabitants to your city. It attracts all of Satan's minions. It invites them to have free reign because they have found a common ground. Satan's greatest connection to humanity is pride. It is the most notable characteristic of his person, and it is the most natural characteristic of ours. If you look at the book of Obadiah, he has lots to say about pride.

> *The pride of thine heart hath deceived thee, thou that dwellest in the clefts of the rock, whose habitation is high; that saith in his heart, Who shall bring me down to the ground? Though thou exalt thyself as the eagle, and though thou set thy nest among the stars, thence will I bring thee down, saith the Lord.*
>
> Obadiah 3-4, KJV

Those who let pride rule in their hearts will be brought low underneath the mighty hand of the Lord. The scripture declares that your pride has deceived you. This word for deception can also be translated as dilution. Pride dilutes the word of God; it makes it weaker in your life. Pride and deception walk hand in hand. Every time you are in pride, you are also in deception. Your pride causes you to manipulate those around you for your own benefit. It causes you to be manipulated yourself.

Your pride welcomes urbanization. It draws everything into the middle of your city and builds the skyline that obstructs your understanding of God. Your pride reinforces the walls of the embassy of offense. Pride will latch onto your offences. It'll hold on to unforgiveness, and it will feel justified in holding on to it. In fact, it will seem that offense and unforgiveness are power that you hold over people, but the only power that's being executed is over you. You're the one in bondage. We need to get free. We need to destroy our idols. We need to destroy the citadel of pride.

Another repercussion of your citadel is the perversion of love. It causes us to view love through our own desires and personal pleasures. It causes us to love with a perverted, selfish, and circumstantial love. It causes us to use people to satisfy our own desires. It causes us to abuse our relationships. In Ezekiel the 16th chapter it references the sins of Sodom and Gomorrah.

> *Behold, this was the guilt of your sister Sodom: she and her daughters had pride, excess of food, and*

> *prosperous ease, but did not aid the poor and needy. They were haughty and did an abomination before me. So I removed them, when I saw it.*
>
> Ezekiel 16: 49-50, ESV

There has been a lot said about Sodom and Gomorrah, and there has been religious tradition abounding in regard to its fall. But the Lord tells the prophet Ezekiel, the exact problem of Sodom and Gomorrah. If you asked most people, they would say it was sexual immorality that led to the fall of the city, but sexual immorality was just a symptom of a far more deeply rooted issue.

We are seeing this symptom all around us in the United States. Alternative sexual lifestyles are abounding, and sexual perversion is everywhere. We've got a whole system built on gender fluidity and lack of categories. It seems like the enemy wants to take all the lines and all the categories and all the differences and uniqueness of people and establish singularity, which is actually a pagan idea that was brought about at the Tower of Babel. But this isn't the base of our issue, just like it wasn't the base of Sodom's issue. Notice what it says in verse 48, the sin of Sodom and Gomorrah was not sexual immorality, it was pride. What I'm saying is that pride causes us to function in those things. Sexuality, love, and identity are all twisted under the influence of pride. Your citadel is casting a shadow over your cityscape. It is causing perversion.

This is all happening because we don't want God to rule our city. We don't want God to overtake our cities with His love. We want to rule our city. We say, "No, Jesus can't have this area of my life. I love the Lord, and I sing to him. I pray, and I talk to Him. I do all of that, but I just believe that love will win. I believe His grace is big enough, and so I don't need to give Him control. God is big enough to just look past my stuff." That's a dangerous place to live. I'm thankful for the grace and mercy of God. I'm absolutely thankful for the preachers that are telling you that God's love is big enough to swallow you up, but if they are telling you that you have no obligation to respond to God's love, then they're lying to you. They're deceiving you. If you're a new creation, you should be walking in new creation realities.

The number one barrier to this becoming a reality is pride. We cannot come to Jesus with pride. We cannot dictate to the master how He is to deliver us. We cannot negotiate terms with the God who created us. When the Holy Spirit moves upon us, it is up to us how we respond. We must respond with humility if we're going to be free. That means that we have to have the humility of mind to state when we are wrong. When we are guilty, and when we need repentance in our lives, we must approach the throne of God. Many times, people want God to release the chains, but yet they do not want to humble themselves before the Lord. There is absolutely no way that you'll receive from the Lord without humility of heart. We are to walk as Christ walked, live as He lived, be holy as He is holy.

These are not popular things to talk about. We'd rather try to maximize our relationships and use our God-given giftings to become successful people. All the while, God wants us to transform into children. This is not a popular message anymore. We want to be a version of Jesus, not Jesus. We want the parts we like. We want Jesus to look like us. This is pride. This was the root of all the behaviors of Sodom and Gomorrah. Pride is what caused it all, an uninvolvement with God. When you are uninvolved with God in an area of your life, you get into error, you get into disobedience, and you get into sin. Pride always leads to destruction, and it always leads to construction. It tears down everything that is beautiful and pure and replaces it with everything that is perverse. It is time to allow the Spirit to invade the citadel.

Section 4:
The Perilous Populace

The metaphorical city of your soul has all of the same characteristics of a physical city. It has its own transportation system, complete with roads, highways, and byways. It has streets that hustle and bustle, and intersections such as the corner of Perception and Reality. It has its own architecture, arts, sciences, and personal proclivities. It has separate city sectors that act as its organizational system. It has seedier, less developed areas that have been neglected because they lack value to you. It has prominent and highly invested areas that lend themselves to the development of your internal culture. It has its own personal memorials built in remembrance of the things and people that we have lost. It has its own history, and its own set of beliefs and values. Along with all of these attributes, it also has its own demographic.

Did you know that your inner city is inhabited by personalities? Now, I'm not saying that you're Sybil and have 101 personalities. What I'm saying is that there are attitudes and inhabitants that run amuck in your city. What would your city be if it didn't have a populace? It would be nothing more than a wasteland. Life is what makes a city run; likewise, our city is full of inhabitants. It is full of people, manifestations of ideas, and spirits. Our city's inhabitants will tell us a lot about how we will respond to the external world around us. Now, these inhabitants are not physical ones. There aren't biological beings walking around in your city. They are mental and spiritual manifestations. Those voices that consistently speak to you, the ones that consistently harass you are the inhabitants of your city. They are there to get you so focused on the Secret World that you abandon the Secret Place. The Secret Place has two inhabitants- you and God. But the Secret World is about you, and you invite all kinds of people and ideas and spirits to occupy the emptiness that a self-involved life leaves you.

You are the star on Broadway in your Secret World. In your secret city, you're the one that is starting for the Yankees. You're the one, until you fall in love or take on a new hobby or are inspired by a new hero, and then you aren't alone anymore. You have a population, and the longer you live, the more your city expands, the more that population grows. The people in your city are drawn by its geography, its personality, and its culture. What we are going to have to learn to do is kick out all of the citizens of our secret cities and get back to a place of intimacy with the Father. We are going to have to evacuate our Secret World, so God can take back control.

This isn't as simple as telling our inhabitants to leave though. This requires us to gain knowledge of the Word, so that we can use that knowledge as a means of power. One of my favorite scriptures in the whole Bible is found in John chapter 17 verse 3. It says, *"this is the way to have eternal life—to know you, the only true God, and Jesus Christ, the one you sent to earth" (NLT)*. The degree to which I'm going to experience life eternal is in proportion to the knowledge of His word that I possess, and the knowledge of kingdom principles that I possess. The word knowledge used here is the Greek word *ginóskó*, which refers to an experiential and intimate knowing. The more I intimately know Him and His ways, the more I experience life eternal. The more I get to experience life eternal, the more I am able to walk free from the confines of my Secret World. This is why it is essential to understand how our Secret Worlds operate.

ME TO THE POWER OF MANY

Your Secret World began with one person in mind, and that one person is you. The initial and primary inhabitant that occupies your city is, of course, you. You build your world around your own experiences, beliefs, and preferences. You have buildings all around that are dedicated to you, and they are filled with all kinds of information that is all connected to you. They are filled with all of your life experiences. In your Secret World, you get to be right all of the time. Your city says that you're right because it's a city named after you. This means that your city trumps other people's. Your city is the most primary and important to you. Within your city, your dreams are housed. Every billboard has your face on it. If you go watch TV in one of those apartments there, it's going to be TV You. It's going to be a You action-adventure film, a You drama, a You sitcom. Guess what? They are rolling out a red carpet out there by Madison Square Garden. And who's walking on it? It's you. You are the professor of every lecture at every college that's in the city. Are you getting a picture? You are the star. The libraries there are about you. Every book is about you. Everything is about you. You are the boss, and the TV star, and the CEO, and the President.

What I want you to see is that the enemy is able to infiltrate and begin to cause strongholds to be stabilized. He uses your own pride and self-involvement against you. He guards your strongholds to where any thoughts, any ideas, any messages, anything of the anointing of God is blocked. He guards you from anything that could obliterate that city by stroking your ego.

This seems like a natural and simple concept, but in actuality, it is quite complex. The complexities of human nature are filled with a variety of nuances. Here is the thing, who you are is not the only part of you that occupies your city because, in actuality, our identity is not just made up of who we are. There is much more to you than that. Your identity is made of who you are, who you think you are, and who you want to be. These people can be very similar, but each have their own set of intricacies that make them independent from each other.

There are also previous versions of yourself that walk around the streets of your city. We are growing and changing all of the time, humans are rarely static. Our lives are dynamic, and they shift and change at a moment's notice. These changes leave many different shells of the person we used to be all over the place in our soul realm.

Different versions of ourselves that interact with each other, that communicate with each other. They often interfere with the person we are now. They often change the trajectory of our path. They change the way we respond to circumstances, and even the way that we define ourselves.

Some of these versions we wish we could have back. Maybe they are the innocent versions of ourselves before we messed everything up or maybe before we got hurt. They are versions of ourselves that possessed qualities that we are envious of, qualities that we wish we still had. These versions make us nostalgic. They make us feel like we will never fully heal, and that we can never have that kind of joy, or peace, or gentleness again.

There are other versions that we are not so fond of. These are versions that haunt us. There are people who look like us that we aren't proud of. People that we can't believe we once were. These are people whose mistakes still bring us condemnation and shame. These are people who existed on the other side of our repentance, on the other side of our growth. The enemy uses these versions of ourselves to distract us from the progress we have made, to distract us from our God-given righteousness. He wants us to step out of our identity and accept our shame.

The people we are, the people we think we are, and the people we want to be are all walking around our city. The various versions of ourselves that we have grown out of canvas the streets. These people all interact with each other, and they all interact with the version of you that is in charge. Like a hundred different voices booming and echoing against the walls of the buildings in your city, these versions can be immensely powerful. They can distract us from the only version of us that truly matters, and that is the version that identifies with Jesus and Jesus alone.

RESIDENTS OF INSPIRATION

Apart from the versions of yourself that occupy your Secret World, you also have many other people that you allow to walk around. The people that have impacted you also have a place in your cities. Heroes, muses and inspirational people living and not living, we can hear their voices in the quietness of our lives. It could be an inspirational speech given at a time of action or the muses of song that succored us through a dark time. Whether prose or performance, these inhibitors direct and busy the mind. If you were to walk around portions of my city, the entertainment district would have the mighty Van Halen playing every night, Jaws would be playing at the cineplex, and the arts district would be flooded with my favorite actors, actresses and musicians. Not as they truly are, but as I see them. That is in regard to me. The arena would have the 96' - 98' Chicago Bulls playing and any other sports team I had made an emotional connection with during my life. The books, movie quotes, speeches etc. that I personally invested in and found to be resonant with my current worldview create the hustle and bustle of my cityscape! Also, relatives that have gone on and are no longer alive on earth inhabit my cosmogony. They are alive and well and are still serving up life lessons. As fun as this sounds it can be detrimental to your life. This can convolute the truth and keep you from finding answers in Christ. The renewed mind has at the center an exalted Christ! He is the source of any and all inspiration and His will, His ways and His words must be the basis for all of our inspired motivations. The wonderful thing is that Jesus uses people, places and things to breathe into us and invigorate us with life! But if those tokens of inspiration are cross grain to the Word of God they need to be evicted out of the city!

Unclean spirits can use these as connection points to begin to influence you to their agenda. I have known many people that have had large portions of their lives impaired by words that they have received from significant people in their lives. It would seem that they never were able to overcome the voices of the past. This goes for personal praise as well as criticism. Both can manipulate and cause you to get off track! I have known of people that still converse with dead relatives and other significant personalities they revere instead of seeking the counsel of God. These entities have nothing new to say, and it is not them, but familiar spirits seeking to deceive and enslave you. Expel them from your city limits and guard against their reentry!

The enemy will look for any possible way to get control of some sector of your city and he will hijack your imagination to do it!

ENEMIES OF THE STATE

Like any physical city our mindscape can be populated with nefarious characters. Ghosts from our past, attitudes and mindsets meandering through the corridors of consciousness. These are the ones we have to continually be on our lookout for. They are conspirators and allies of the enemy of our soul. They seek to give entrance to the tactics and wiles of the devil. We police them through renewing our mind with the Word of God and being spiritually aware through prayer. We can only successfully apprehend and eliminate these menaces to our mental health by subjecting them to the truth of God's Word and our obedience to it!

"Having purified your souls by your obedience to the truth…"
1 Peter 1:22 ESV

It is the passion of our flesh that gives birth to these cretenets of confusion. Our fleshly lusts and desires also energize this populace to cataclysmic proportions.

"Beloved, I urge you as sojourners and exiles to abstain from the passions of the flesh, which wage war against your soul."
1Peter 2:11 ESV

These perpetrators hate your obedience to God's Word, and by doing so, you subject them to judgement that incarcerates and expels them from your metropolis!

These enemies of the state can walk around unnoticed and inconspicuous at times, but when lust is active, they go in full riot mode railing against the truth of God's commands! They seek to overthrow any and all revelation that you have acquired and dispel any confidence in the Word of God. When these characters rear their ugly heads, seek to banish them from your city by repentance and prayer. Accountability will also aid in keeping them from reentering the city limits

Section 5:
Invaders from Outer Space

The previous section refers to the inhabitants that you willingly invite into your city. These are the people that you give permission to be a part of your world. They are people who reside in your city because you put them there, people you love, people you hate, people you admire. They are ones you have connections with, and the ones you have willingly given a say in your life, but apart from these every day, run of the mill, inhabitants of your city, your Secret World is also filled with a criminal element. Believe it or not, your city's streets are filled with gangs and ruffians. They are filled with uninvited inhabitants. These citizens are not ones that you have willingly allowed to take residence in your Secret Worlds, but they came to infiltrate and begin new works in your city sectors.

We will call these unwanted visitors invaders from outer space.

GATEWAYS INTO THE CITY

The front gate of your city is your permission. When things and people come through the front gate, it is because you gave them access to it. This is the only way that Jesus will enter your heart. In John's Revelation, Jesus says,

> *Behold, I stand at the door and knock. If anyone hears my voice and opens the door, I will come in to him and eat with him, and he with me.*
>
> Revelation 3:20, ESV

He is a gentleman and will not enter your city without your permission, but evil spirits do not have this same respect. For the most part, people do not willingly invite evil spirits in, so they have to look for alternative means of entrance. There are many things that can open up alternative gateways to your city. These gateways act as secret passageways that allow the enemy access to your Secret Worlds. Now, we have already discussed how hurt and loss can cause your walls to be broken down. A breached wall is a surefire way to allow the enemy access, but there are also things that can build alternate gateways that give any number of spiritual entities the ability to influence you from the inside out.

The first alternative gateway is anxiety. Anxiety is a state of worry, unsteadiness, or nervousness. This is one of the most common gateways that people absentmindedly build into their city walls. Anxiety, as a mental health issue, affects more than 40 million adults every year in the U.S. alone, and that is just people who have sought medical help (ADAA). We know that anxiety is not of God because in Philippians 4 verse 6 it commands, *"do not be anxious about anything"* (NIV). If God commands us through His holy scripture to not do something, it is a good indication that it is not God's will for us to deal with it; however, most people still struggle with anxiety in one form or another. One of the most notable scriptures about anxiety is found in Proverbs.

Anxiety in a man's heart weighs him down, but a good word makes him glad.

Proverbs 12:25, ESV

The word used here for *weighs* is the Hebrew word *shachah,* which means to cause someone to bow to a higher power. What does anxiety do? It forces us to worship a false god, to elevate our circumstance, and its perceived outcome, above God. Worship to false gods is an open invitation for them to enter into our Secret Worlds, thereby creating a gateway.

Another thing that opens up backdoors into your city is discouragement or disappointment. These emotions occur when hope is delayed or shut down. When we expect a situation to go one way, but it instead goes another. Discouragement and disappointment aim to rob us of our joy. Without joy, the believer has no strength.

> *Hope deferred* (or discouragement) *makes the heart sick: but when the desire comes, it is a tree of life.*
>
> Proverbs 13:12, NKJV

The word used for *sick* here is the Hebrew word *chalah,* which means to be worn down until weak or to become sick unto death. The enemy uses discouragement as a tool to wear away at you. You can start out completely confident in hope and anticipation, but through repetitive discouragement you get worn down. This wearing away makes you vulnerable and susceptible to the enemies' attacks. When a discouragement or disappointment is dwelt on, it opens the door for the enemy to attack.

Another gateway into the city is anger. Now don't misunderstand. Not all anger is bad. There is a righteous anger that is accompanied by a holy zeal. This is the anger that Jesus showed when he flipped the temple tables in Matthew chapter 21; however, it is rather rare that you see people angered by sin. This is because most Christians are at peace with their sins. Righteous anger is used for the benefit of the kingdom. The majority of people experience unrighteous, uncontrolled anger. Instead of using their anger for the benefit of the kingdom, they allow their anger to use them to benefit destruction. The enemy wants to use your anger as a gateway, as a secret passage that gives him an invite into your Secret World. Psalm 37:8 says, *"stop being angry! Turn from your rage! Do not lose your temper—it only leads to harm"* (NLT). The command here is to refrain from anger and to turn away from rage. The consequences are clear: it only leads to harm. In other versions it says, "it only leads to evil." Anger leads us into evil. It invites the enemy in, and sustained anger invites him to remain.

It is important for us to understand that anger is not a primary emotion. This means that there is typically an underlying root emotion that is causing you to respond in anger. That might be hurt, pain, or insecurity. These emotions are under the surface, and when they are incited by a word from a colleague or a verse in the Bible, the enemy tries to get you to tap into the secondary emotion of anger. He wants to use this as an open door. He antagonizes you. The initial word might not have been that bad, but then he prys and taunts. He mocks you and manipulates you until the rage builds and becomes unreasonable. You lose control, and the anger takes over. All of a sudden you start seeing red, and you say things that you don't mean. You become vengeful, and out of your mouth, you align yourself with the enemy's agenda. That alignment opens up a gateway and sends out an invitation.

Another thing that opens a massive gateway into your city is fear. I have heard it said many times that fear is the antithesis of love. And if this is the case, that means that it is the biggest enemy of love ruling and reigning in your life. 2 Timothy chapter 1 verse 7 lays this out pretty clearly saying, "for God has not given us a spirit of fear, but of power and of love and of a sound mind" (NKJV). The spirit that God has given us, the Holy Spirit, is in stark contrast to fear. Fear is not in our gifted spirit. In fact, "fear not" is the most common command in the scriptures. This is because fear is the direct enemy of love, and God is love, so, in turn, fear is an enemy of God. This is a rather simple concept, but still, our lives seem to be so completely racked by fear. How are we supposed to combat an emotion that is so primary to people who know so little for certain?

> *do not fear, for I am with you; do not be dismayed, for I am your God. I will strengthen you and help you; I will uphold you with my righteous right hand.*
>
> Isaiah 41:10, NIV

The reason we should not be afraid is because He is with us. He is our God, and we are His children. He is a faithful God, so that means that He is watching over us. He has built a hedge of protection around us. Our confidence is in the Lord. When we surrender our minds and emotions to fear, it is an indication that we are no longer reliant on Him, that we aren't trusting in Him. The root of this is the question of who God is or how much He cares for us. We should not embrace anything that makes us question who God is, and when we do, just like Eve in the garden, it opens the door for the enemy. It gives him and sin a place in our hearts. It opens a gateway that is not easily sealed up.

Jesus is referred to in scripture as the Prince of Peace, so if we have a revelation of who He truly is, then an aspect of our worship to Him should be to remain in peace. When we remain in peace, these alternative gateways into our cities are locked up. They are sealed so that the enemy is stripped of his backdoors. When we do not remain in peace, it opens up gateways that invite unwanted visitors into our cities. This can be detrimental to us because these unwanted visitors can become citizens that manipulate and influence us from the inside out. Our job, our goal, is to know God because when we know Him, we are granted the ability to remain in perfect peace.

SPIRITUAL VAGABONDS

If I asked any of you to close your eyes and imagine a big city, many of you would have similar images that popped into your heads. You might imagine booming streets, large buildings, and art. You might imagine a coffee shop on every corner, or a hot dog stand parked at the intersection of Main and First. If I asked you to imagine the people of this city you might picture men in suits walking around with their briefcases clutched closely to their sides, or street vendors trying to push their wares. Many of you would imagine one or a few homeless people meandering about. This is one of the first images that would be brought to my imagination. In my experience with major cities in the United States, homelessness is a typical and prominent characteristic. The larger the city, the more massive the homeless population. This is primarily because those without homes are drawn to places with lots of inhabitants. This is because they typically have more freedom amongst the masses and a greater access to resources.

The homeless population of our Secret Worlds are what is referred to as transient thoughts. Now these are thoughts that don't initially seek to make a home in your city. They are just passing through. They are like spiritual vagabonds. They are hurled at you as burning arrows. They come to see if they can materialize into something more. They come to your city seeking out an opportunity, and if they don't find any, then they are on their way to the next; however, when they do find the opportunity they are looking for, they decide to set up tents and camps. They begin to establish temporary residence in order to lay the foundation for evil spirits to reside more permanently.

The enemy hurls thoughts and accusations against you just to see if one will stick. He commissions spirits to release vagabond thoughts to meander through your city, just to see if they can find a place to rest their heads. And if he throws one that doesn't stick, he waits a little while and tries again later. He waits until you are in a vulnerable state, and then throws one again.

He uses these thoughts against you. You begin to think it's you. You begin to think it's your observation, and that it's your thinking. When we hear something enough times, we begin to think that it's our thought. You may be a married man, but one day at work, a beautiful woman walks in, and an inappropriate thought is hurled at you. Then you think, "Oh, my God, where did that come from?" "I must be a horrible human being; I must be a horrible man." You start to feel guilty and ashamed. You need to throw those thoughts out and replace them with thoughts that are righteous. But then you see another beautiful woman, and another thought is hurled at you. You begin to rehearse your guilt and shame all over again. You think that you are just a terrible, no good man. No, that thought came to you from a spirit.

If you get a hold of this, you will experience so much freedom. If you are in Christ, you are righteous! This means that any thought that is contrary to Christ is not a part of your nature. I can hear the shackles falling now. I can feel it. This will set you free. You see, your spirit is your communication device with the spirit realm, that means that your voice is going to be the voice that you hear. This confuses many Christians. This is why so many believers think that God isn't speaking to them. They expect an audible voice. They expect Morgan Freeman to come on a loudspeaker and tell them what to do. That is not how God chose to interact with us though, and that is not how other spiritual beings interact with us either.

Let me give you an example: I'm a demon spirit. Now don't take that literally, but just as an example. What I want to do, what I have been commissioned to do, is bring division between you and your friends. I will cast a thought at you that your best friend doesn't really like you anymore. Although the evil spirit is the one who whispers that transient thought to you, you receive the thought in your spirit, so when it comes to your mind, it sounds like you. It is modulated to fit your voice. Spirits continue to hurl these ideas and thoughts at you until they can persist in your mind. The goal is to not be homeless anymore. These spiritual vagabonds may come in as drifters, but they don't want to stay that way. They come in as hobos. They have their little knapsack, and they are just looking for a place to spend the night. If you let them stay for the night, then they want to build camps. They want to find a way to make themselves more comfortable, and once they build camps, they want to build more permanent residence. Their goal is to build a permanent residence so that the spirit that released the thought can become a permanent citizen of your city. They want a place to reside, a place to call their home.

And so, they try to see if they can get something to stick. They try to get you to camp out on a thought. They are looking for whatever you will give them access to. Now, ultimately, the choice is completely yours. You have to make a decision whether you are going to take a hold of that thought. You determine how long these drifters stay. You can lay hold of that thought and cast it aside, or you can meditate on it. If we start rehearsing these thoughts and giving ourselves over to them, we give them residence. We give these vagabonds room to build when we begin to ponder on them, when we begin to lend substance to them. You begin to act on those thoughts, allowing them to lead you into doing things you would not otherwise do.

What's happening? That hobo, that transient thought is spreading his cardboard box out in your head. He is getting his little rotisserie out, and his dog is messing all over your sidewalks. The more you meditate on it, the worse it gets. Some people's cities have a Skid Row. They have entire sectors that have been overrun by transient thoughts, and they just let them make their home right there in the middle of their cities. They create little zones of dependency where they suck up all of your city's resources, where they take all of your energies.

This is exactly what these transient thoughts aim to do. They get you worked up and emotionally supercharged. They get you pacing back and forth meditating on the perceived slights from friends or imagined betrayals from a family member. Then it turns into this huge fight that comes in to bring division, and when it all comes to a head, the enemy has done exactly what he has purposed to do. He released a drifter into your city to try and bring division. You gave it place. You rehearsed it, and you gave it residence until it materialized into something real. We let it materialize into a residence for spiritual entities to make their home inside of. We must be on guard against these thoughts. We must cast them out of our cities. We must guard ourselves against replacing our parks with Skid Rows. Be on guard and cast out the drifters before they set up their tents.

THINGS THAT GO BUMP IN THE NIGHT

The demonic entities that surround us are constantly in communication with us, and we respond to this communication so naturally. When demons of depression attach themselves to us and whisper our worthlessness in our ears, we respond out of our own mouths by confirming their opinion. When demons of sexual immorality attack, we respond to them and confirm their position when we let our minds undress our coworkers. When Christians speak anything that is contrary to God and their identity in Him, then it is abundantly clear that they are being manipulated by voices not their own. Evil spirits are releasing those transient thoughts and sending them as scouts into your city. But once the residence is built by those thoughts, then the enemy has even more say in your Secret World. Once they are permanent residents, they have more influence. This is because when you are a citizen, you get a vote. Citizens get to influence a city's decision making.

Something goes bump in the night. You hear a rustling in your closet as you try to fall asleep. You hear a door creak shut. As children, these signs indicated that there was a boogeyman coming to get us, a monster that was trying to take us away in the night. When we were younger, our moms and dads used to tell us that we were overreacting. They told us that there were no such things as monsters. When we thought something was under our beds or in our closets, they would tell us it was in our imagination. They would reassure us that monsters didn't exist. Our guardians wanted us to be safe from our worries and fears; however, as we get older, we begin to realize that there are monsters. The spiritual world and even the physical world are filled with monsters. These monsters may be people who have done terrible things, or they might be spirits who have rebelled against God. Either way, they are very real. They exist all around us, and the greatest of these, the most detrimental monsters, live in your head. They inhabit your Secret World. These monsters seek to maintain control of your psyche, to manipulate your purpose, and to keep you from the presence of God.

If you have ever seen *Star Wars,* you have a pretty good physical representation of what is happening spiritually all around us. The humans in Star Wars live side by side with all kinds of beasts and monsters. For the most part, they are not in conflict with these beasts, but they live in harmony and communicate with them naturally. This may seem like an outlandish example, but in actuality, it is what we are experiencing daily. If we could see what takes place in the spiritual realm, then we would be shocked by how accurate this depiction truly is. The spiritual realm is very real and vibrant. We interact with it on a day to day, moment to moment basis. We are driven by it, tempted by it, and overwhelmed by it. Our Secret Worlds are created by its influence. The spirits that we interact with on a daily basis want to make a home in our Secret Worlds. They want to create a place where they can exist without any risk of being removed. They want to acquire voting rights, so that they are not just influencing you mentally, but they are influencing you physically as well. In the last portion, we discussed our city's vagabonds, transient thoughts, but what happens when those thoughts make space for the monsters?

    Your Secret World becomes flooded with invaders from outer space. These are persons without bodies, also known as unclean spirits. Transient thoughts make homes for unclean spirits. They clear out a space and make room for these spirits to probe you.

HIERARCHY OF THE MILITANT MINORITY

These invaders from outer space become your city's criminal presence. The more power you lend them, the more powerful the criminal presence in your city. This criminal element can cause you to do all kinds of things both internally and externally. Just like any successful group, there is an organization to their authority. If someone walked up to you in normal clothing and commanded you to do something, you probably would just disregard them; however, if they were to come up to you in full military regalia and bearing weapons, then you might think twice. Why is that? Because a man is just a man, but when he is backed by a nation, a military, he has the power of that nation backing him. This is because organizations carry more power than individuals. Where there is order, there is influence. Satan knows this just as well as anyone. Due to this, there is a spiritual hierarchy that has been established in the second heaven, the realm your Secret World exists in. At the very top of this organizational structure is Satan.

you were dead in the trespasses and sins, in which you once walked, following the course of this world, following the prince of the power of the air, the spirit that is now at work in the sons of disobedience.

Ephesians 2:1-2, ESV

Here, a title is given to Satan. That title is *the prince of the power of the air.* The word used for *prince* is the Greek word *archón*, which means the first in authority. We are well aware that Satan doesn't have more authority than Jesus, so then by process of elimination, it is clear that this means he is the supreme authority over the fallen spirits that reign in this world. The word *prince* is dependent on what follows. He is the prince of the powers. The word for *powers* is the word *exousia*, which refers to the delegated spiritual influences. In this verse we learn that Satan is the highest level in the hierarchy of invaders, but he is not the only rank. There are three other levels of power mentioned in scripture.

For we do not wrestle against flesh and blood, but against the rulers, against the authorities, against the cosmic powers over this present darkness, against the spiritual forces of evil in the heavenly places.

Ephesians 6:12, ESV

This verse shows that we are not struggling with flesh and blood. Our fight is not against what we see or experience with our senses. We can get this mixed up all too often. We see a political figure that stands contrary to the things of God, and we begin to bash them. We begin to criticize, but when we are made aware that our battle is not with them, then the strategy behind our fight shifts completely. Our battle is not against the ones we see. Our battle is against the spiritual hierarchy. It is against the spiritual invaders that manipulate and persuade those we see. As Christians, we need to stop fighting the battle in front of us and start fighting the war that is raging all around us.

This verse goes on to establish the three structural classifications of evil spirits that we are called to wrestle against. The first being rulers. The word for *rulers* is the Greek word *arché*. This word has the same origin as the word *prince* mentioned previously. This word refers to the highest rank in our militant minority. It is the principality, the chief. These are demonic forces that reign over entire nations. They influence and lead the nations that they are over.

The next level is authorities. This word applies to spiritual entities that have been given the right to reign over regions or cities. They have jurisdiction inside their domain, and their influence is attached to their domain. In order to understand this one, I always picture a police officer. When I am in Tulsa, OK, and I see an officer from Mannford, OK, I am not afraid they are going to pull me over and give me a ticket because they are outside of their jurisdiction. They have no authority in Tulsa because they are not a Tulsa officer.

The next level is the level that we deal with most frequently. This is the level that interacts with us personally. The criminal element that wreaks havoc in our cities is the *kosmokraters*. These are the enforcers. Principalities and Authorities don't seek permanence in our Secret Worlds. They aren't seeking citizenship because our personal lives are small potatoes to these guys. The powers, however, seek to dominate and control us. We will refer to this final group as the mental mafia. They are intent on gaining power, and their only access to power is through individuals. The demands come down from the top, but the war is fought from the ground up. Nations can't be influenced, unless individuals lend their authority. Towards the beginning of this book, we discussed that Satan's primary objective is to create cosmopolis. He wants to create a one-world system that he rules over, a world irrespective of God. This is what he hoped to accomplish through the city of Babel. He wanted to convince people that they didn't need a God, but this is just a guise because what he really wanted was to manipulate them into bowing their knees to him. The mental mafia might as well be Satan's errand boys. They are sent to disrupt your life, so that your authority can be siphoned from you.

Your mental mafia seeks control. These unclean spirits have two objectives. They want citizenship, and they want dominance. They bully and manipulate their way up through the ranks of your city. They try to limit all the other voices that have a say in your life, so that they can control your thoughts and actions. Their ultimate goal is a complete city takeover. They don't just want to be your city's criminal element, but they want to be your city's militant government. They aren't satisfied with oppression alone. They will fight for dominance. They will fight for possession of your Secret World, a complete militant takeover.

GANGS IN THE STREETS

Since these spirits are the low man on the totem pole, they aren't super powerful, but that is exactly why they don't work alone. This is a tactic you see often in the wild. Wolves are a great example of this strategy because they are not especially strong. They are not the biggest predator, and they aren't the smartest. What they do have, however, is a pack. They can take out a bear even though the bear is much larger and much stronger because they aren't alone. They run in packs because in numbers, there is strength. This is how the mental mafia works too. Demons come in gangs because the spirit on the inside of you is much bigger and stronger than them. One on one, you could easily stand against them, but when they attack, they do it in hoards, and these hoards overwhelm the average believer.

Remembering back to the story mentioned in Mark 5, the Demoniac of Gadara was not just possessed by one individual unclean spirit, he was possessed by many.

> *For he said unto him, Come out of the man, thou unclean spirit. And he asked him, What is thy name?*

And he answered, saying, My name is Legion: for we are many.

Mark 5:8-9, KJV

When Jesus asks the spirit his name, the response is *Legion*. This word refers to a regiment of the Roman army, which usually numbered about six thousand persons. Now if the unclean spirits were being literal, this implies that the man's Secret World had been overrun completely by evil spirits. His city's streets were taken over by an insurrection of invaders. He was consumed by gangs of strongmen that forced him to screech, to self-harm, to break chains, and to torment those that surrounded him. He was bullied by these spirits into doing their bidding. He mustered up the last bit of control he had to run to the feet of Jesus, and that final act of freewill set him free.

This may seem like a farfetched example. From our experience we don't encounter many people who have been possessed by a Legion of unclean spirits; however, this is what the end of the road looks like. This man didn't start his journey with six thousand spirits reigning as the criminal element in his city. No, just like all of us, the attack starts with a transient thought. It begins with a word being hurled at us over and over again until it sticks. It starts with probing and poking, testing to see for weak points, and then when one is found, it opens up a gateway and prepares a home. It gives the enemy place, and then one by one they come, and when there are enough unclean spirits and strongmen walking around in your Secret World, they plan an insurrection of mass proportions. They instigate a complete city wide take over.

This isn't a rare occurrence. Far more people are oppressed by demons than we are aware of. If you are sick in body or sick in mind, then there is a good possibility that you are being afflicted by an evil spirit. If you are constantly doubting yourself, or you find yourself in condemnation, then there is a good chance you are being oppressed by an evil spirit. I am not saying any of this to scare you. Contrarily, I am actually saying this to set you free. There is freedom for those who know they are being afflicted but how? How do we combat these invaders from outer space? We see in John that Jesus had it figured out. He was not influenced by any evil spirit, but just the spirit of God. In this verse Jesus says,

> *The prince (evil genius, ruler) of the world is coming. He has no claim on me. [He has nothing in common with me; There is nothing in me that belongs to him, and he has no power over me].*
>
> John 14:30, AMP

The enemy had no hold on Him, but how did He get to that place? The key is found in Matthew.

> *Then Jesus told his disciples, "If anyone would come after me, let him deny himself and take up his cross and follow me. For whoever would save his life will lose it, but whoever loses his life for my sake will find it. For what will it profit a man if he gains the whole world and forfeits his soul? Or what shall a man give in return for his soul? For the Son of Man is going to come with his angels in the glory of his Father, and then he will repay each person according to what he has done. Truly, I say to you, there are some standing here who will not taste death until they see the Son of Man coming in his kingdom."*
>
> Matthew 16:24-28, ESV

The key to your freedom is simple. Whoever will lose his soul (world-city) will find life! The word soul here applies to your mind, will, and emotions. It refers to everything that is influential and created in your cities. When we hold onto these things, it is our responsibility to make sure things run correctly, but when we surrender them all to Him, He is able to purify them. When we make Jesus the supreme authority of our soul realm, the enemy no longer has any place.

This might seem like an overly simplified solution to spiritual oppression, but it is true nonetheless. I remember hearing a testimony at a conference that really put it into perspective for me. The man who was speaking was an Indian who converted to Christianity from Hinduism. His conversion story was quite interesting, and it has always stuck with me. If you don't know much about Hinduism, let me give you a brief overview. In the Hindu religion, there are three main gods, and then many lesser gods that are worshipped. Most families also serve a family god. This is a god that receives personal worship and servitude. When the speaker at this conference was younger, an evangelist came and taught him about Jesus. After much consideration, he decided to give his life to the Lord of lords, Jesus. When he went back home, his mother was sobbing uncontrollably. He had thought that someone had passed away, so he asked his mother what was wrong. His mother responded, "our god left us." When he asked her to explain she said, "he packed his bags and told her that Jesus lived there now, so he had to go." When the man submitted himself to the lordship of Jesus, Jesus took complete control of his life. His presence cast out the presence of every other spirit.

No god can stand in the presence of the one true God. Surrendering yourself completely (your thinking, your choices, your feelings) to Jesus will set you free. It is a beautiful paradox. Lose your Secret World, and you will find the Secret Place.

LOOTING AND RIOTING

All of your inhabitants, the perilous populace and the invaders from outer space, work together in your city. These imaginative manifestations of the people you are and have been, of the people you know, are all manipulated by the enemy to enforce control over you. The spiritual entities that have made their way into your Secret World are in this same business. They are all a part of the demonic system that wants to keep you living you-centric life. They want to keep you in slavery to sin by keeping you in bondage to yourself. They want you to live from your Secret World and to surrender your access to the Secret Place.

Let's look at some examples of this. Let's take a real sticky issue, tithing. That's really sticky for a lot of people because when you're approached with the truth, you get slammed by the enemy. A minister comes up and starts talking about tithing, and immediately your city starts lighting up. You may have gone to a church that said tithing is not for the New Testament believer or a church that abused their stewardship of finances. When that minister is up on stage, the enemy is right in there, all of the manifestations and spirits are in the streets, and they are rallying. They are crying because the truth has happened. You will always know when truth truly shows up because your city will be set ablaze. When your streets are burning, you know the truth has been presented because it compromises your inhabitants. It compromises their position in your soul, so you start hearing "preachers are liars, they only want your money for a hot tub." Your city just lights up with all of these lies. Your inhabitants start throwing bricks in the streets and setting things on fire. Your financial district is under attack. Someone gets on stage and starts explaining tithing to you in the nicest way possible, all the while your inner world is raging. The truth is that tithing will really help you, and it'll set you free from the bondage of your finances. But on the inside, you are saying "I can't believe he's saying that." "Down with tithing!" There is a huge riot on the inside of you. That's when you should know, if you're wise, that the truth has been presented.

This same thing happens with sex. Let's take the truth that premarital sex is sinful. You hear a preacher say that you should walk in purity, and your inhabitants start acting foolishly. You hear God said be holy as I am holy, and all of the sudden puritanical culture is bondage. The voices rally, telling you to relieve yourself from the patriarchy. That flesh gets energized. You start kissing your girlfriend, and then all of the sudden the Holy Spirit puffs up and says, "be holy, even as I am holy." You are presented with a choice, and your city rises up. "The Bible's not real." "That's not the real word of God." "You just need to do whatever you feel like doing, so you can be happy." And all of the sudden you are willing to compromise for a couple of minutes of pleasure. Like Esau, you are willing to sell your birthright for a bowl of bean soup (Genesis 25) all because the city rages. When we step over into what we're being tempted to do, we feel relief. There's a certain type of pseudo peace that we experience, but it's a false freedom.

You know exactly what I am talking about. You've seen some of the riots and things that have been on our news and on our social media pages, and some of the videos of all the chaos. That is exactly what starts happening in your Secret World. All these little ideas and transient thoughts that you've let in because of your lack of discipline begin to run rampant. You haven't girded up the loins of your mind, you haven't set yourself to be active in your mind, so you just let information come in. You don't care what it is, and you don't disseminate it. You rarely take the time to put it underneath the microscope of the Word of God. You just take it in whatever *Disney* says. You take in whatever *CNN* talks about. We are lackadaisical, and we do not guard ourselves. We just take it all in, and it makes us vulnerable. It causes us to be taken into captivity by keeping us from the truth.

> ,,,If ye continue in my word, then are ye my disciples indeed; and ye shall know the truth, and the truth shall make you free.
>
> John 8:31-32, KJV

The more we take in, the more reinforcements the enemy has. The more inhabitants he can use to strongarm us into obedience. The whole time we think we are living in freedom, but the residents of our city are really in control. The voices that are in opposition to the truth stand up and protest and fight back because they don't want you to be free. They don't want the Holy Spirit to use the truth to set you free, so they try to separate us from the word. They loot and riot to keep you from continuing in the only thing that has the ability to truly set you free.

Section 6:

Hardened Hearts of Concrete and Steel

It is important to be aware of the fact that not everything that happens in your life causes things to be created in your Secret World. There are many people that you interact with that will never make their way into your heart. There are many words you hear that simply, as the saying goes, go in one ear and out the other. There are instructions that take place that you completely rebel against, and you refuse to harbor within yourself. There are many events that you let roll off of the shoulder. There are many temporary buildings that go up in your city that are demolished and replaced rather quickly. Not everything becomes detrimental, so then what is it that causes things to be cemented and set in stone? What is the difference between something that is temporary, and something that is concrete? How does something become real to us? How do we determine whether or not it is permanent? The answer lies in our partnership. What we choose to partner with, what we choose to come in agreement with causes concreting to take place in our Secret Worlds. We are making *concrete* decisions that will build something, and if we don't deal with it spiritually, it becomes permanent.

What does this look like in real life? You get married, and you think it should be this wonderful Walt Disney style situation. You imagine that it is going to be this beautiful fairytale that people talk about for generations. I am sure this is what my wife imagined before we got married, that is the dream that most young girls imagine. But you quickly realize it's more horror than Disney. Now, don't misunderstand. This is not the case for everyone, but more often than not, this is what happens. People expect it to be rainbows and butterflies all of the time. They expect love and passion to be a part of their everyday lives. Why would we even get married if this wasn't an aspect of what we were anticipating? But anyone who is married knows that there are aspects of it that aren't very pretty, that aren't very good. This person, the one you chose, has basically been selling you that they're the best person on the planet Earth, but that can't last. You have been deceived. People can't put on their best face all of the time, and they quickly turn into something different after you get married.

There are a lot of people that have realized too late that they have made a bad decision, and instead of letting God come in and provide a solution, they are trying to make it work. Satan wants to build something in your life to impair you and handicap you. He wants you to settle for something that seems right in your own eyes. He wants to keep you from achieving God's objectives for your life, and he does this by causing things to become concreted in your Secret World.

When you enter a marriage without the full knowledge of what you are getting into, it can swiftly become terrible and hinder you from achieving your purpose in life, hinder you from walking in joy. You are so focused and wrapped up in how bad it is, you settle in every other area of your life. You don't have any energy to heal the other places of your life because you are putting all of that energy into fighting and bickering. What you have done is you have come into agreement with something, in this case someone, who is detrimental to your walk with the Father. You were convinced that it would be a good thing, that it would be a beautiful thing, but you didn't see the full picture. You didn't see that you were making an agreement with an entire other world. When we make covenants like marriage, we take on all of the other person's struggles and doubts. We take on all of their spiritual attacks and mental deficiencies. When we come into agreements with ideas, circumstances, or people it is very similar. What we make "truth" to us becomes concrete. What we decide to agree with causes our hearts to be hardened by the solidification of our cities.

The hardening of our hearts is the solidification of our Secret Worlds. The more expansive and real our Secret Worlds become, the harder our hearts get. The harder our hearts get, the more real the repercussions.

WATCHING ASPHALT DRY

Many of us have allowed things to concrete inside our Secret Worlds that are detrimental. We have come into agreement with people, things, and ideas that keep us from experiencing the heart of God for our lives. The contractors come in and start laying concrete, they start hanging steel, and they start erecting buildings. They take what you have agreed with and give it permanent placement in your Secret World, in your internal city, and your hearts become hardened. Slowly, but surely, our hearts become stone. Ephesians chapter 4 verse 18 says,

> *They are darkened in their understanding, alienated from the life of God because of the ignorance that is in them, due to their hardness of heart* (ESV).

Let's spend a little time unpacking this scripture. It is apparent from this text that when our hearts are hardened, it causes alienation from the life of God. The word here for alienation is the Greek word *apallotrioó,* which implies estrangement. We are rendered disconnected from the Father, when our hearts are hardened. It causes us to be unable to participate in fellowship or intimacy. This is more than just being shut off from the intimacy of God. It also breeds ignorance. It stirs *agnoia,* which is a refusal to know real truth, a willful blindness. When our hearts are hardened, we are darkened, or morally and spiritually blind, in our understanding. Understanding here refers to the ability to draw divine conclusions. Our disconnection from the Father limits our ability to make progress and experience personal breakthroughs. Here it is clear that hardened hearts have a great deal of repercussions. They cause spiritual blindness, willful ignorance, inability to make progress, and a lack of personal, intimate relationship with God. If these things are not dealt with, we will not see the goodness of God unfold in our lives, and we will not be conduits by which the spirit can establish the Kingdom of God in the earth.

When we allow ourselves to construct an entire world inside of us, complete with roads, architecture, and inhabitants, it severely limits us. When our Secret World causes our hearts to be hardened with permanent and solidified structures, it changes the way we see and interact with God and the world around us. When Pharaoh's heart was hardened, he was unable to listen to reasoning, and he refused to let the Jews in Egyptian captivity leave. This led to the death of his firstborn son, and the death of countless others (Exodus 7). When the disciples' hearts were hardened, they were unable to calm the storm. This caused them to completely give into fear and panic (Mark 6). If Jesus wasn't with them, it could have potentially led to the death of everyone on their boat. When King Belshazzar's heart was hardened, it caused him to lose his throne, and eventually the glory of God departed from him (Daniel 5). He lost his ability to lead and to experience God because his heart was hardened, because his Secret World was being cemented inside of him.

It is so important to realize the spiritual effects that a hardened heart has on us. Firstly, it limits our ability to hear clearly from God. On many occasions during my 20 plus years in ministry, I have heard people tell me that they don't know how to hear from God. You may be thinking the exact same thing right now as you read. I remember many instances in my life when I was frustrated because it seemed like everyone around me was hearing the voice of God besides me. What I didn't realize then is that God is always speaking. He wants intimacy with us, and He always has the line of communication open. Notice that when the

Heavens opened at Jesus' baptism, they stayed open (Matthew 3). There is no scripture that says, "and then they closed back up." No! They were opened, and they are still open to this day. The divine conversation that Jesus initiated is perpetuated by the Holy Spirit in every moment. The problem is not on God's end. It is on our end. God desires us to communicate with Him, and He is always speaking. The problem is that when our hearts are hardened, we are unable to hear and understand His voice. In Matthew 13 verses 14 through 15 this truth is reiterated,

> *...You will be ever hearing but never understanding; you will be ever seeing but never perceiving. For this people's heart has become calloused; they hardly hear with their ears, and they have closed their eyes. Otherwise, they might see with their eyes, hear with their ears, understand with their hearts and turn, and I would heal them* (NIV).

This scripture reveals that those with calloused or hard hearts will not be able to see or hear spiritually. Even though the Lord is constantly speaking to us, and constantly revealing things to us, when our hearts are hardened, we are unable to truly understand what He is saying and revealing. Their callousness has caused them to *hardly hear* and to *close their eyes.* If their hearts were not hard, they would be able to understand. This understanding would lead to their healing or their *iaomai,* which refers to a restoration of wholeness.

Apart from a lack of understanding, hardness of heart also causes apathy. Apathy is a dangerous place to be. Our indifference towards people and the things of God is a massive indication that our hearts have become hardened. We lose our passion, and we become stagnant. When water becomes stagnant, it causes it to be a breeding ground for bacteria and many dangerous ailments. Drinking stagnant water can cause serious harm to our bodies. When the well of life that is on the inside of us becomes stagnant, the same thing happens. We become overcome with sickness down to the very core of our beings. This causes a lack of joy, peace, and contentment. It makes us numb to the world around us, and it causes many people to fall into a depression. This state removes people from the presence of God by causing them to disregard Him. In Romans 12:10-12 it says,

> *Be devoted to one another in brotherly love. Outdo yourselves in honoring one another. Do not let your*

zeal subside; keep your spiritual fervor, serving the Lord (BSB).

It goes on to say in this same chapter that this is what allows us to overcome evil with good. We are commanded to keep our zeal and spiritual fervor, but this is impossible to do when our hearts are hard.

Our hardened hearts also cause us to doubt the supernatural. I think it is very obvious that we experience less of the supernatural than what we see in the book of Acts. Many Christians have made excuses for this, claiming things like "the supernatural was just for the early church;" however, this is far from the truth. In fact, the presence of God and His miraculous works are even more accessible to us. He has poured out His Spirit on all flesh, and where His Spirit is, there is potential for power. The problem is not that we don't have access to the supernatural, but that our hearts have become hardened, and it limits our ability to see the supernatural take place. In Mark chapter 6 we see that the disciples struggled with hardened hearts too. It says in verses 48 through 52,

> ...he saw that they were making headway painfully, for the wind was against them. And about the fourth watch of the night he came to them, walking on the sea. He meant to pass by them, but when they saw him walking on the sea they thought it was a ghost, and cried out, for they all saw him and were terrified. But immediately he spoke to them and said, "Take heart; it is I. Do not be afraid." And he got into the boat with them, and the wind ceased. And they were utterly astounded, for they did not understand about the loaves, but their hearts were hardened (ESV).

Let me set up this picture for you. The disciples had just witnessed Jesus feed approximately twenty thousand people with 5 barley loaves and 2 small fish. Not only did they all eat until they were full, but they also had 12 baskets of food left over. This is a crazy miracle that they got to witness. They got to participate in carrying this miracle out. It happened through their own hands. But when we find them just a couple of verses later, they are completely shaken by the miraculous. As a matter of fact, they don't even recognize Jesus. They are terrified of Him, and they even think He is a ghost. When He proceeded to calm the storm, they were *astounded*. Let me remind you, these men walked with Jesus every day. He had calmed the storm before. He had fed thousands of people with less than an adequate amount of food. He turned water into wine. He raised people from the dead, but they were still *astounded*.

Many of us are still astounded when we see God's miraculous power. When we witness something supernatural, we are in a state of ecstatic shock. This is very natural, but did you know that this is not the proper response? Our response should not be one of shock, it should be surety. If we are truly standing in faith, the supernatural should not surprise us. The supernatural is a natural repercussion of our intimacy with God. So, why are so many people shocked when they see miracles unfolding? Well, the answer is in this passage, "their hearts were hardened." When our hearts are hard it causes us to doubt, and it limits our ability to operate in faith. A soft heart expects miracles. A soft heart walks in faith.

Most Christians are unaware that they have lived their entire Christian walks with hardened hearts. They are unteachable, unable to understand God, apathetic, and they doubt the supernatural. Many don't realize that these things are symptoms of a hardened heart. They have never made the diagnosis, but when we come into agreement with the enemy and help him solidify things in our Secret Worlds, the result is a heart that has been hardened. The enemy has come in and laid asphalt, built architecture, and invited inhabitants. We have come into an agreement with him and lent him our authority, and we have an entire world to show for it. We have an entire inhabited city that runs and operates apart from God, and it is holding us back.

HEARTS THAT MELT LIKE WAX

When we begin to come into agreement with the things in our Secret Worlds, permanent structures of concrete and steel are created within us, causing a hardness of heart. We have discussed the effects of a hardened heart, the results of our Secret Worlds' solidification. When hearts are hardened, words cannot penetrate them, and doubt rises within them. Your enemy is banking on the solidification of your Secret World because he wants to keep you from experiencing God. He wants to keep you from bringing His kingdom into the earth. We have already built so much in our Secret Worlds. We already have a bustling city on the inside of us, so what are we to do? Do we just try to live our lives without expanding the city? No, just like the enemy can use your agreement to build cosmogony, God can use your agreement to tear it down. He wants to reestablish the Secret Place inside of you. He wants your heart to be a temple that He can inhabit.

So then, the question is: how can this be accomplished? The natural approach is to isolate a problem and attack it head on. You would think that going to each individual piece of architecture and tearing it down is the solution. You might think you need to go to each person in your Secret World and kick them out one by one, but that would be a tedious, time consuming, and discouraging approach. Many people think that focusing on the problem is the only way to solve it, but on the contrary, focusing on the solution is a much more enjoyable and lasting approach.

You can spend a very long time chipping away at an iceberg, but then you just have a whole lot of snowflakes. If you want the things of God to flow from your life like a mighty rushing river, then you shouldn't waste time chipping away at an iceberg, you should just push it in front of the sun. We don't want a heart filled with shaved ice; we want a heart that has a powerful river flowing from it.

> *And I will give you a new heart, and a new spirit I will put within you. And I will remove the heart of stone from your flesh and give you a heart of flesh.*
>
> Ezekiel 36:26, ESV

This scripture lays out the solution perfectly. Our new heart is a gift from Christ. We receive it from our union with Him. The process of allowing our hearts to be overtaken by the Spirit of God requires us to turn our gaze towards the Son. When we set our gaze towards Him and increase our proximity, then our hardened hearts will naturally melt. Just like natural substances, the harder the material the higher the melting point. If you are looking to melt an iceberg, you only need it to be about 33 degrees fahrenheit. If you are looking to melt wax, you need it to be about 115 degrees fahrenheit. And if you are looking to melt concrete, you are going to need it to be about 1832 degrees fahrenheit. The harder the heart the more exposure to the Son that is necessary for their hearts to be softened. This process can take some time, but it is so worth it. Save yourself some time and heartbreak. Don't focus on the problem, don't focus on the sin, don't focus on the city, focus on Jesus. He is the solution. Revelation 1:14 says "He has eyes of fire," and when we gaze into those eyes, our hearts have no option but to melt.

Although this seems simple, many people don't know how to gaze. I want to give you a few practical tips that will help you transfix your gaze on the solution.

> *Lord God, unlock my heart, unlock my lips, and I will overcome with my joyous praise! For the source of your pleasure is not in my performance or the*

sacrifices I might offer to you. The fountain of your pleasure is found in the sacrifice of my shattered heart before you. You will not despise my tenderness as I humbly bow down at your feet.

Psalm 51: 15-17, TPT

Proximity requires humility. David depicts this perfectly. He wants his heart to be unlocked, he wants his hardened heart to be softened, so he brings his heart before the Lord. He shatters it at His feet. He comes to God in complete humility and willingness to be changed however God sees fit. God sees this as a pleasing sacrifice. The fountain of His pleasure is the sacrifice of humility. You are not good. You are not even okay. You can't do this on your own. You don't have the answer, so stop trying. Present your life to God, broken and contrite, and watch what He can do with it.

Have you ever looked through a window at the sun? It is a little hard to do, but ultimately the sunlight just filters through the glass. There may be a minor reflection that bounces off of it, but for the most part, the sunlight just comes through the glass from one side to the other. But when you break the glass, when it is shattered into a thousand little pieces, the sun is filtered through it. It reflects off of the pile of brokenness in a beautiful plethora of ways. When we are whole, Jesus' light can illuminate us, but when we are broken, it can reflect off of every little piece of brokenness and illuminate the world in beautiful manifestations of His grace. God needs you to be broken. He needs you to present yourself to Him in humility, not because it benefits Him, but because it is the only way that He can use you.

Another thing that helps you to set your gaze on His purifying eyes is the cultivation of intimacy. In the passage from Psalm 51 mentioned previously, David bows down at God's feet. This is a sign of closeness. If you are not close to someone, you do not have access to their feet. If we think about the woman with the issue of blood that is mentioned in Mark 5, we see that she had to fight through a crowd of people to close the gap between her and Jesus. She had to be close to Him to touch the hem of His garment, and she had to touch Him to be made well. Likewise, the wellness of our hearts is contingent on our proximity to Christ.

The most effective way to cultivate intimacy is by developing a disciplined prayer life. In your relationships, the more you communicate with someone, the closer you get to them. Your communication opens up the door for you to experientially know someone. You get to know their beliefs, their interests, their passions, and ultimately their hearts. Our communication with Jesus does the same thing. It allows us to know Him intimately, but this conversation requires discipline. God is a quality-time God. We must set aside time to be with Him. I have counseled many people over the years. Many come with serious problems that they want to overcome. Problems with their marriages, problems with addiction, issues with sins, and many with other difficulties. Whatever the problem, one of the first questions I ask them is: how is your prayer life? The truth is that most people have a severely malnourished prayer life. If you dedicate 10 minutes to Jesus, and then wonder why you aren't experiencing the realities of the kingdom in your life, then you have your answer. Without prayer there is no breakthrough. The problem is that most people are too lazy to cultivate a healthy prayer life, and so they do not experience any real intimacy with God. It takes time, discipline, and practice to learn how to pray. It takes work to cultivate intimacy, and most people are not willing to put in that work.

We interact with God and seek His face in the same way we interact with the world around us. We take Him in. We engage with Him. This is easier to do with the world because there are so many methods by which we can engage with the world and culture. We can watch TV. We can listen to music. We can play sports or go on dates. We can look at art or read books. All of these things help us to interact with the world around us, and these can all become methods by which we interact with God too. We just have to change what we are looking for. If our heart's desire is to find God, then we will find Him in every part of our lives.

Humility and intimacy are two things that are absolutely essential to cultivate in order to gaze upon the eyes of Jesus. Without these things our hearts will stay hardened and calloused. God wants to penetrate our calloused hearts, but it requires us to respond to Him the way that King David did. We must come to His feet with broken and contrite hearts.

Section 7:
City Shakedown

I understand that all of this is just a concept at first. It only becomes real when we acquire true revelation, when we choose to put faith behind it. Unfortunately, sometimes this doesn't happen until we are forced to rework it, until we are forced to reevaluate and perform a complete city overhaul. It becomes real to us when we have to put these things into practice in our own lives, for the sake of our own lives. As a pastor, I've helped many other people over the years go through serious situations in their lives, but I personally had never been touched with anything that was considered life threatening until November 11th, 2018. It was my granddaughter's birthday, and right after the party, I was rushed to the emergency room. Earlier that day, I began to notice that I was carrying a lot of water weight, and I had recurring symptoms that I kept trying to fight off. When I arrived at the hospital, I was found to have water building up all over my body. I did not have any answers as to what was going on at that time, but they eventually found that my heart had gotten down to 15% capacity, and that 15% capacity had been weakened even further by a virus. Just like that, for the very first time in my life, I was fighting for my life, and what I realized in that moment was that I had no clue how to fight.

Through this process, I began to see that even though physical things contributed to my weakened heart, spiritual things were the root cause. I had harbored hurt, unforgiveness, and bitterness and each of these things shared authority in my Secret World. They had each become solidified, and they were hardened through concrete and steel. They began to build structures, and they influenced the appearance of portions of my heart. They obstructed my view of the Father and opened up gateways in my city that allowed the enemy access into my life. I did not know at the time, but the enemy came in and put weedkiller on everything that was organic in my life, everything that was pure. He ran interference between me and God.

Through this process, God began to teach me what fighting this battle entailed, and what He showed me was that it required a complete overhaul. This means that He has to trample and put to dust your high and lofty buildings. He has to destroy the highest edifices and the highest places in your life. God wants to trample down and totally destroy and annihilate everything that is contrary to His kingdom. He doesn't want it in your life anymore, but we try to preserve those things. We try to look at their validity thinking there's some good stuff in our cities. You just know that there are some good deeds, some properties that have value. However, even my exhibition of fleshly morality can also be based on pride because my dependency isn't on God. My dependency is reliant on myself to keep rules.

If you think this process is going to be neat and tidy, you are in for a rude awakening. This overhaul is going to be messy. It is going to require some dirt on your streets because when God deals with your pride, when He deals with that center thing that's attracting the enemy, it is going to be painful because we're partial to our city. We give guided tours showing off its cityscape. We're proud of it. It is my city, my place! I reign supreme, but then God begins to deal with it. He begins to bring in His bulldozers and the deconstruction crew that are His ministers. This will be painful, but if you want true life, if you want the life that you're supposed to have, you're going to have to give Him a permit. You're going to have to open your gates, and you're going to have to let the wrecking ball in.

CITY STANDSTILL

In a previous section we discussed how Cain, after he was cursed by God, left his homeland. Where did he go? He went and built a city. Cain was cursed to become a wanderer, but instead of getting down on his knees and asking for forgiveness, he decides to rebel again and create a city. He did what any fallen, prideful human being would do. Instead of humbling himself and asking God for mercy, he created a system in his mind to override the curse. This is exactly what we find ourselves doing. We get in trouble. We experience a trauma of some sort. We find ourselves deep in sin, and instead of getting down on our knees, we start building things to protect or validate us. We start establishing roads, systems, and architecture. We start picking and choosing who we let into our hearts, and we make sure that all of it serves our own interests. We think "I'm going to guard myself. I'm going to protect myself. I'm going to keep myself secure." All the while, we are building a prison that keeps us from feeling life. We have got to end this cycle. We have to stop the perpetuation of construction in our Secret Worlds.

We need an absolute city standstill. We must stop all permit issuing and real estate bartering and cease to give place to the devil!

We need to stop the commotion and progress of our cities. In order for us to enter into a process of deconstruction, and eventually restoration of The Secret Place as the center of our lives, we must first bring the traffic, the construction, and the hustle and bustle of our Secret Worlds to a complete halt. We have to stop running. We have to stop our wandering, and we must begin to humble ourselves and seek the Lord. This can be a difficult task for us because culture is quite contrary to this idea. It is egocentric and individualistic. Our culture is high intensity and fast paced, but that is not the way to the heart of God. He wants us to build from a place that is contrary to our culture. He wants us to build from a place of peace and rest, a place of reliance and humility.

> *Be still, and know that I am God: I will be exalted among the nations, I will be exalted in the earth.*
>
> Psalm 46:10, ASV

This verse is one of my favorites in the whole Bible because it contains so much depth in such a simple phrase. It is a bipartite scripture. The first part is to be still. The second part is to obtain the knowledge that He is God. What most translations fail to convey, however, is that the second part is actually dependent on the first. A more accurate translation would be "Be still to know that I am God." This scripture isn't giving two commands. This scripture is explaining that the only way for us to know that He is God is by being still. The word used here for *be still* is the Hebrew word *raphah*. This word means to fall limp and become helpless. So, what is a city standstill for the realm of our souls? It is a state of complete surrender. It is a place of helplessness and reliance, a place where all of our strivings cease, and we lean into God completely.

This concept seems counterintuitive to many of us with a western mindset, but the way of the kingdom is often paradoxical. When we make ourselves aware of our helplessness, we receive help from the King of all nations. The ways of God are often contrary to the ways of the world. We must give to increase (Proverbs 11:24). We must lose our life to gain it (Luke 17:33). The last will be made first (Matthew 20:16). Those who make themselves helpless will receive help. This scripture lays out the precedence for great breakthroughs. It demonstrates the necessity we have for a city standstill. The knowledge of God is essential if we want our Secret Worlds to be flipped upside down, but in order for us to obtain this knowledge, we must first take a pause.

> *Then you will know the truth, and the truth will set you free.*
>
> John 8:32, NIV

Know the truth, and the truth will set you free. Jesus is the way, THE TRUTH, and the life (John 14:6). If knowing the truth sets us free, and Jesus is the truth, then knowing Jesus sets us free. A key is given here: humble yourself, become helpless, and you will know God. Knowing God provides freedom from the confines of the self-imposed prison we have come to know as our Secret Worlds.

This is a relatively simple concept, but yet it is extremely challenging because we want to encounter God in our own way. We want to negotiate the terms of our relationship with Him, but it is so audacious of us to attempt to enter into negotiations with the God of all creation. He is not open for negotiations. He sees what we cannot see and knows what we cannot know. An overhaul of our Secret Worlds requires us to surrender our *absolute yes* to Him. It requires us to fall limp in His presence and acknowledge our helplessness. We cannot do it on our own. We needed a savior. God provided that savior. Now we need to take a note from Jesus' beloved disciple and lean against His chest so that He can explain the mysteries of His divine sociopolitical order, so we can know how to replace our Secret Worlds with His Secret Place.

THE DECONSTRUCTION CREW

In God's divine justice, He has chosen to limit His own sovereignty. He chose to give humanity the mandate of reigning and ruling on the earth. Since the beginning of the Bible, God has always chosen to move and operate through man. He has chosen to partner with us in the establishment of His kingdom on the earth. This approach has not altered in regard to how He has chosen to deconstruct and replace our Secret World with The Secret Place. He has put together a deconstruction crew that is equipped with all of the tools necessary to rework your city. This crew consists of the 5-fold ministry roles and the wrecking ball of the Holy Spirit.

Each of the ministry gifts play an important role in the process of deconstructing and replacing your Secret World with The Secret Place. If you are not familiar with the reference to the 5-fold ministry, they are found in Ephesians the 4th chapter.

And he gave some, apostles; and some, prophets; and some, evangelists; and some, pastors and teachers;

                              Ephesians 4:11, KJV

The first gift mentioned is the Apostle. This word derives from the Greek *apostolos,* which translates to a *sent one.* This is someone who acts as a delegate of the gospel message. They carry the message on behalf of Christ, as an ambassador does. The role of the Apostle is to grow the church through the establishment of new works. They are especially gifted in awakening us to our God-given purpose. They have the ability to speak life to the visions that God has placed in an individual's heart. When we partner our purpose with the gift of the apostle, we are awakened to our true identity and given direction on the path set before us by the Father. This may not seem to make sense in regard to the replacing of your Secret World, but the discovery of your purpose and the vision that God has for your life is essential. It gives you an insight into your God-given identity, and the apostolic gifting has the ability to walk beside you in the fulfillment of your destiny.

The second gifting listed is the prophetic office. The word used here for *prophet* is the word *prophétés*. This word can also be translated as *poet*. The derivation of the word *poet* can be traced back to *one who creates*. The implication here is that the prophet has the ability to exposit divine truth. The role of the prophet is to use their voice to bring spiritual truths into the physical realm. Prophets have the ability to search the heart of God for His people. Through their interaction with His heart, they are able to uplift and direct His people. They can help the believer affirm things they have heard and begin to recognize the voice of God. A word from God created the Heavens and the Earth, and a word from God can replace the world that is inside of you too.

The third gifting mentioned is the role of the evangelist or the *euaggelistés*. These are people who operate as messengers of the Gospel, these are also known as missionaries. They bring the joy and the testimony of the Lord with them everywhere they go. They are a living, breathing invitation to know the Father. Evangelists are passion bearers, and they stir up a curiosity and a desire to know Jesus more intimately. The evangelist benefits us by drawing our attention towards the Father. They remind us of what Jesus did for us, and when we partner with this gift, we are humbled and inspired.

The next role presented is the pastor. This is more accurately translated as a shepherd, poimén. Shepherds are in charge of a flock or a group of people. Pastors are the gift that has the most influence and the most direct access to your Secret World. They hold a major role in the deconstruction and reconstruction of your soul. They are directors that guide people through their brokenness and show them the way to restoration. Shepherds correct us, they direct us, and they feed us. They have constant input in the replacement of your Secret World. It is absolutely essential for us as believers to submit ourselves to a pastor because they are gifted with the ability to see what we cannot see. They can work in tandem with the Holy Spirit to dissect our lives and bring about internal restoration.

The final role mentioned is the teacher. Teachers, *didaskalos*, are masters of specific topics. They illuminate the word of God and the person of Christ. They bring understanding, and they make truth and knowledge more readily accessible. Teachers are gifted to confront lies in our Secret Worlds, to cast down the enemy's attacks. They can bring the truth when it seems far, and the truth has the ability to set us free. When we partner with teachers, they help our lives to reflect the scripture. Their instruction helps us to become disciples that have fruit evident in our lives.

These gifts were given to us to benefit and empower us. The previously mentioned passage goes onto say that they were given to us:

> *for the perfecting of the saints, for the work of the ministry, for the edifying of the body of Christ: till we all come in the unity of the faith, and of the knowledge of the Son of God, unto a perfect man, unto the measure of the stature of the fulness of Christ:*
>
> Ephesians 4:12-13, KJV

The first thing these ministry gifts were purposed to do was to perfect the saints. This doesn't mean that they are supposed to make the individuals within the church perfect. What this really means is that they were given to work out the saints, to get them into shape. They are meant to help believers become servants of the Gospel and of Christ. They lift us up, so that we may become people consumed by Christ. They lift up the church by lifting up the individual. They teach us what it means to be a disciple. They build us so that we can live with constant access to the Secret Place. The Holy Spirit works with each of these giftings to wreck the things that we have constructed in our soul realm. He comes in and interacts with the inhabitants and deconstructs the architecture. When our worlds are deconstructed, these giftings then begin to work with the Holy Spirit to allow the organics of the Spirit to prevail in our lives.

UNATTENDED OVERGROWTH

Have you ever been intrigued by landscaping? As I have traveled abroad, I have noticed something that perplexes me as I peruse highways and byways, neighborhoods, and subdivisions, it is their landscaping techniques or lack thereof. Now, this may seem insignificant, but in some places of the world, the evidence of their lack of upkeep is everywhere. The grass grew wherever it wanted. The trees reached over the roads in the most inconvenient ways. The animals grazed without restrictions, and the differentiation between the rural and the urban was opaque to say the least. This was something that was completely foreign to me, and it seemed irresponsible and lackadaisical to my western mind. However, some cultures, especially Meso-American countries, have a distinct purpose for it. These people believe that nature should not be restrained, and that man did not have the right to confine what God decided to grow.

Now, don't go telling your wives you didn't mow the grass because you didn't want to restrict God. That is not the purpose behind sharing this analogy at all. The reason I share this is to point out the spiritual truth it revealed. The Secret Place, the place God wants us to live from, is organic.

It is full of lush grass and thick forests. It contains no urbanization. It is a Garden of Eden for the soul, an oasis. Nevertheless, true to our nature, we try to restrain and constrict what God wants to grow inside our souls. This is the way of the fallen, depraved man. In this present age, I hear God calling us back to the garden, inviting us back to intimacy.

He wants to establish in you an incomprehensibly beautiful paradise, but there are some things about this paradise that we must understand if we want to live from it. First, we must understand that the Secret Place is God-centric, so it is time for a Coup d'état, a total government overthrow. You, your loved ones, your idols can no longer be on the throne. It is time to remove all leadership and establish Christ as the one true King in your heart. God has declared Him the rightful ruler. In Psalm 2 it explains,

> *For the Lord declares, "I have placed my chosen king on the throne in Jerusalem, on my holy mountain."*
>
> Psalm 2:6, NLT

If we want God to establish His Holy Place in our hearts, then we must also accept His chosen King. There is no King more worthy than He. When we live lives that are dedicated to ourselves and our own vain pursuits, we find ourselves in depressive states. We become empty and overwhelmed by the culture of the world. But when we submit ourselves to His leadership, we are given the promises that accompany Him as our great Shepherd.

He makes me to lie down in green pastures; He leads me beside the still waters.

Psalm 23:2, NKJV

Establishing Jesus as our King and Shepherd ensures that we will be protected from harm and provided for. He will make us lie down in green pastures. He will lead us beside tranquil and peaceful waters. When we operate in the Secret World, we are led and motivated by a monarchy that is composed of our own pride and conceit. When we operate in the Secret Place, we are led and motivated by a monarchy of truth and purity, and when we become captivated by this monarchy, it changes the geography of our hearts completely.

Further, we have to grasp that the Secret Place is not just about us and God. It is about the Kingdom of God, and it is centered around the objectives of God and truth. When you surrender yourself to God, you must be willing to be used by Him. As mentioned in the previous sections, God has chosen to partner with man. In His perfect justice, He has chosen to limit himself. In love, He has chosen to enter into a covenant relationship with mankind. Due to this covenant, nothing, absolutely nothing, can be accomplished in the earth until a man or woman of God moves. His kingdom will not come, and His will can't be done until we are in a position to be used by Him. Entering into the Secret Place ensures that we are in that position, but with that placement, we discover that it takes a great deal of self-sacrifice to be a conduit of Kingdom objectives. In John, Jesus lays out exactly what this requires of us.

> *This is my commandment, that you love one another as I have loved you. Greater love has no one than*

this, that someone lay down his life for his friends. You are my friends if you do what I command you.

John 15: 12-14, ESV

When we are living from the Secret Place, we are given the capacity to love one another, but the validation of this love has a stipulation attached to it. This stipulation is to lay down your life. The word used here for *life* is the Greek word *psuché*. This word means soul life, which is our Secret World. In order for us to love one another, we must lay down our Secret Worlds. Our inner world incapacitates us. It takes away our ability to love others properly, but when we lay it down and take up the Secret Place the overgrowth of the spirit empowers us to love.

The Secret Place also has guarded borders. When we reside in the Secret Place Jesus builds a hedge of protection around us.

The angel of the Lord encamps around those who fear him, and delivers them.

Psalm 34:7, ESV

You hem me in, behind and before, and lay your hand upon me.

Psalm 139:5, ESV

For he will hide me in his shelter in the day of trouble; he will conceal me under the cover of his tent; he will lift me high upon a rock.

Psalm 27:5, ESV

When we live in the Secret Place, we are protected. We are guarded in the day of trouble. When we fear God, He commissions an encampment of angels to protect us. He hems us in. This is a glorious promise, but it doesn't seem as wonderful as it is. This is because His protection also demands holiness. It calls us to a standard of righteousness. When we begin to operate from the Secret World, some things begin to grieve our spirits that didn't before. There is painful refinement that comes because love demands a standard. When we don't stand in that standard, when we start to let things that are contrary to God back in, then our Secret World begins to build all over again. The hedge is there to protect His investment.

> and give no opportunity to the devil. Let the thief no longer steal, but rather let him labor, doing honest work with his own hands, so that he may have something to share with anyone in need. Let no corrupting talk come out of your mouths, but only such as is good for building up, as fits the occasion, that it may give grace to those who hear. And do not grieve the Holy Spirit of God, by whom you were sealed for the day of redemption. Let all bitterness and wrath and anger and clamor and slander be put away from you, along with all malice. Be kind to one another, tenderhearted, forgiving one another, as God in Christ forgave you.
>
> Ephesians 4:27-32, ESV

In this passage, we are commanded to give no opportunity to the Devil. We are commanded to not grieve the Holy Spirit that lives on the inside of us. The border that surrounds the Secret Place allows us to feel when the Holy

Spirit is grieved. It provides us with a deep conviction when we are outside of God's will. This can be painful and uncomfortable at times, but it keeps us from giving opportunities for the Devil to reconstruct our Secret Worlds.

The Secret World is soulical, but the Secret Place is spiritual. The process of deconstructing our Secret Worlds is challenging. It is painful and tedious, but it is so worth it. The spiritual is green. The spiritual is organic. It is natural. It is substantive. It lacks carnality. It requires much of us, in fact, it requires all of us. It demands a standard. It demands that we lay down our lives for our brothers and sisters. It demands that we give ourselves so Kingdom objectives can be established in the earth. But it also provides us with an identity that is not dependent upon others. It provides us with a joy that is uncircumstantial. It provides us with a hope that cannot be shaken, and most importantly, it provides us with an intimacy that invites us to reside in love. If you remember nothing else from this book, I pray that you remember this. A life surrendered to God is the only one worth living. You will experience hardships. You will experience sickness and pain, but you will live the life God intended for you to live, and you will be fulfilled.

Beloved, I urge you as sojourners and exiles to abstain from the passions of the flesh, which wage war against your soul.

1 Peter 2:11, ESV

If we're going to be successful in this life, we need to be sojourners. We need to be in exile. We need to be pitching tents and building altars instead of the other way around. That means you have no roots. The reason why Abraham went around in tents and did not build a city is because this was not his home. The whole reason why you are filled with fear and can't go to bed at night, and the whole reason why you can't stand the fact that you might lose something is because your roots are too deep in this world. Jesus teaches that the more stuff you have the more pain you have. You're to live as a sojourner. That means that your cities have to come down. The freedom that you are experiencing to your flesh is bondage to your spirit.

Looking at Isaiah 26:1-6 we can see the effect Jesus has on our city when He is allowed access.

"In that day this song will be sung in the land of Judah: We have a strong city; he sets up salvation as walls and bulwarks. Open the gates, that the righteous nation that keeps faith may enter in. You keep him in perfect peace whose mind is stayed on you. Trust in the Lord forever, for the Lord God is an everlasting rock. For he has humbled the inhabitants of the height, the lofty city. He lays it low, lays it low to the ground, casts it to the dust. The foot tramples it, the feet of the poor, the steps of the needy."

Isaiah declares a future song of the land of Judah stating that they have a strong and safe city. How? He goes on to say God has set up salvation which is the Hebrew word Yeshua which is the name of Jesus. This city is safe because Jesus is set up as the ruler of it and He is the walls and bulwarks that protect the city. The text states that we are to open our gates and allow the righteous nation to come in. In Psalm 24 we are admonished to open "wide our gates" so that the King of Glory may enter into our city! It is only when we allow Jesus to rule and reign in our soul that we can experience the perfect peace that is brought forth in this passage. It is through our constant developing trust in Him that we begin to see the destruction of the citadels of pride, monuments of trauma, and the architecture of disobedience.

Jesus will come in with His wrecking ball and lay low to the ground and cast it to the dust all of the things that the enemy has sought to build in your city. The establishment of Jesus as King of your city and Lord of your soul establishes the Secret Place as our center of identification and being. But in order to do this we will experience loss.

Jesus declares that if you're going to follow Him, you're going to have to disregard your own rule over your soul. Most people don't want to disregard themselves. The word that is really used here in the Greek is to utterly deny, to totally forsake. He's talking about forsaking yourself and your city, abandoning it. Let the growth of God take it over. Have you ever seen a city or a town that has been given up? What happens is that the organic growth takes over, and the city starts deteriorating. The man-made structures begin to fall. This is what the Spirit needs to do. We need to allow for rain. We need the Spirit of God to overtake our city, to where it begins to totally deteriorate. What has been built by a satanically inspired system, that I have received and operated in, that has contributed to the way I think and the way I speak, must be torn down.

It is time that we humble ourselves. It is time that the church becomes transparent again. It is time that we open up our hearts and become vulnerable, so that the Father can deconstruct what a lifetime of disobedience has built. We don't get to control it. We don't get to dictate how it happens. The Father is the great contractor, and He wants to release His Spirit in your life. He wants to release a river of life right through the center of your city. He wants the vines of the spirit to overtake every building and sidewalk and monument. He wants to dispel all of the voices and occupants that are contrary to His. He wants to set you free, but this project requires that you sign the permits.

Return to the Secret Place.

He that dwelleth in the secret place of the most High shall abide under the shadow of the Almighty. I will say of the Lord, He is my refuge and my fortress: my God; in him will I trust.

Psalm 91:1-2, KJV

If you have never accepted Jesus as your Lord and Savior and you want to take that step, then just pray this prayer:

Jesus, I believe you are the Son of God, that you died on the cross to rescue me from sin and death and to restore me to the Father. I choose now to turn from my sins, my self-centeredness, and every part of my life that does not please you. I choose you. I give myself to you. I receive your forgiveness and ask you to take your rightful place in my life as my Savior and Lord. Come reign in my heart, fill me with your love and your life, and help me to become a person who is truly loving—a person like you. Restore me, Jesus. Live in me. Love through me. Thank you, God. In Jesus' name I pray. Amen.

Welcome to God's family! I am excited that you have made this very important decision and I pray that your new life in Christ will become a great testimony for our Lord.

Now What?

If you just prayed a sincere prayer of faith and you're wondering what to do next as a new Christian, check out these helpful suggestions:

- Salvation is by grace, through faith. There's nothing you did, or ever can do, to deserve it. Salvation is a free gift from God. All you have to do is receive it!

- Tell someone about your decision. It's important that you tell someone to make it public, secure, and firm. Find a brother or sister in the Lord and tell him or her, "Hey, I made a decision to follow Jesus." Tell someone today if you can. It's a great way to seal the deal.

- Talk to God every day. You don't have to use big fancy words. There are no right and wrong words. Just be yourself. Thank the Lord daily for your salvation. Pray for others in need. Seek his direction. Pray for the Lord to guide you daily with his Holy Spirit. There is no limit to prayer. You can pray with your eyes closed or open, while sitting or standing, kneeling or lying on your bed, anywhere, anytime.

- Find a church and get plugged in somewhere.

ABOUT the AUTHOR

Greg V. Hurd is Senior Pastor of Lake Church in Mannford, Oklahoma. As a Pastor, Greg has a heart to communicate the gospel in a creative way. He began Lake Church in 2007 with a vision to make disciples and to raise and develop leaders for the local church. Pastor Greg is a visionary and is passionate about reaching the world for Christ.

He has been married to his wife Karen for more than 35 years. They have four sons and 6 grandchildren and currently live in Oklahoma.

ISBN 978-1-7378124-1-8